# BLOWING THROUGH THE THICK BLACK SMOKE

By

Dr. Ricky Brathwaite

ISBN 9798305881813

**This project is made possible in part**
**by the**
**Cultural Industries Development Fund**
**Of The National Cultural Foundation of Barbados.**

Published by: XL-ONE PUBLISHING
Tel: (246)547-9657(246)249-7025
E-mail: xl1.publishing@gmail.com

Edit ,Layout, graphic by Margo Durant-Callender

Cover design by Brian O'Neal

Dedicated to

*My small nuclear family: Debbie, Myles and Saniya – my wife, son and daughter, respectively, and a true inspiration for the writing of this book*

Love you all very much!

# ACKNOWLEDGMENTS

I must first acknowledge my God, Father and Savior, Jesus Christ for giving me the Gift, strength, skills and talent to write this memoir of my life's journey to this point.

Cover Design & Artwork: Brian O'Neal

Editing etc... : Margo Durant-Callender

Foreword: Eddy Grant

Cover Photo: Steven Cumberbatch

NCF

All book photos compliments: Ricky Brathwaite Library

# PREFACE

## DR. RICKY BRATHWAITE

I grew up a poor little black boy from the City of Bridgetown in Barbados, in the Caribbean, who rose from humble beginnings to touring and performing the trumpet with Caribbean and international musical greats to achieving the status of doctor.

These travelling experiences and working with the greatest in the Caribbean and North America have impacted my life, not only from a cultural perspective, but from a moral and spiritual one as well.

This book is a mere snapshot of the events that have made my career a delightful one, while presenting some of the challenges encountered along the way that gave me the perseverance and resilience to carry on.

It also examines how I incorporated other skills and gifts as survival tools in the roles of: teacher, tutor, lecturer, composer, arranger, producer, singer and karate expert - hence, the book title: "Blowing through The Thick Black Smoke"

# FOREWORD

Of all the instruments that constitute the modern Symphony Orchestra, I would hazard a bet that the most difficult to master and play with a high degree of proficiency, especially from a tender age would be the trumpet. This could be ascribed to the very limited nature of its construction relative to the range of sound and emotive quality required of it. In other words, at the beginning and for many a year later, both the player and the listener go through an unimaginable amount of aural hell, in the case of the unfortunate listener, and what can only be described as physical torture worthy of that experienced by a practicing Shaolin monk. The thing about all of this is that the young perspective candidate has no idea of the bargain he/she is about to enter into. It's a relationship wherein your partner demands that you proverbially make love every single day and should you miss one single day you'd feel some degree of physical pain, and it doesn't care how "talented" you are or become, the trumpet remains your master for life or for as long as you want to make sweet music together.

I have been privileged to know and to hear some of its greatest exponents and the truth be told, after a certain point, climbing the ladder of technique leads to nowhere but to a kind of proverbial "Babel." By which time, not only has the player/s not met God, but found that the player being worshipped as the deity has found the true way to connect to fellow humanity, a whole different algorithm, that if you'll forgive me, I shall take the poetic license and call it

"HEART." It is not perfection personified, but at its best it has the capacity to make you laugh, cry, and bring forth the entire plethora of human emotions that humankind has been blessed with. So what about Ricky Brathwaite? Oh I err! Doctor Ricky Brathwaite, to give full deserved handle to his already truncated name.

We met, and have continued to do so, under full musical respect. While not seeking to steal his thunder in any way, as this is his telling of his story, one of which I am proud to have been a significant part of for a protracted period of time. I have never, unlike so many of my Caribbean people, subscribed to the "who is best syndrome" which can sometimes hinder development and stop us learning from each other. But on the many occasions that I have needed to have a trumpet on a recording, it would have to be Dr. Ricky. Why? Not just because of his crazy ability to play at hypersonic speed and mind-boggling height, but because of that intangible thiñg that resides in his playing. I call it SäF, it's not Jazz or Caribbean/Jazz or any other phony construction of our peculiar historic patrimony. It's ours.....play it Dr. Ricky play it.

SäF for Life.

Ringbang For Life.

*Eddy Grant.*

**TABLE OF CONTENTS**

# INTRODUCTION

First, it is important to explain how my given name Wycliffe, evolved into "Ricky", and eventually became a household name in Barbados. It also commanded some degree of attention and respect, particularly around the Eastern Caribbean and the Brooklyn, New York area.

The name, Wycliffe was given to me by my late, mother, Joyce Elaine Brathwaite. Wycliffe, was initially pronounced, Wick-cliff, often referred to by my mother as Wic-key, and hence the misunderstanding of pronunciation evolved into, Ricky. This is the name most people have known me as, from as long as I could remember. In fact, very few people are aware of the name Wycliffe. My stage name naturally evolved into, Ricky Brathwaite. I have been asked, on several occasions, if it wouldn't be more pragmatic to change the name on all of my documents to Ricky, but there are a lot of documents that would have to be changed. I, therefore, stuck with my given name, Wycliffe, and my stage name as Ricky. I also thought that Wycliffe was the name given to me by mother, and I should respect that.

# Chapter 1

## HUMBLE BEGINNINGS

I grew up in a small village in the city of Bridgetown in Barbados called, New Orleans. On occasion, I would stay at my father's two sisters' home in Bank Hall. Straddling between these two villages helped to shape me into the person I am today.

In New Orleans, I witnessed what real love was. My mother technically raised me without a father. My father would show up on occasion and when he did, he spoke few words. He would spend short periods at home and would be gone again. I do not remember he and I, ever engaging in the shortest of conversations. My mother was forced to play both roles of mother and father.

My father was the Regional Musical Director of the Salvation Army Band. He played several instruments very well and was very knowledgeable in music theory. In fact, he conducted trumpet classes at the Salvation Reed Street hall, in which I was privileged to attend, and those sessions were extremely significant to my early musical development.

As was earlier mentioned, my brother, mother and father played in the Salvation Army Band. In fact, on occasion when band members did not turn up for Sunday church sessions, those family members constituted the band. I knew that someday I would be a part of the band as well, in whatever capacity.

## Play What?

My parents would on occasion, bring home their brass instruments, either to practice on or to clean. The horns my brother, mother and father brought home were the tenor horn, euphonium or cornet. My mother would constantly remind me that I was not to touch them. She would repeat this several times and state clearly that she did not have the money to fix them should they be damaged. I listened and obeyed for a while. I always wondered, though, how I would ever learn to play an instrument if I were not allowed to touch them.

One day when my mother left for work, I took up her tenor horn and tried to produce a note. I was always curious as to how anyone could produce different notes on an instrument that only had three valves/pistons. I blew into the horn and all that was produced was the sound of wind. There was no sound of a note. I quickly shifted to the cornet, but got the same results. I tried again on the cornet the next day and faintly produced a sound, but a slightly distorted one. I became more and more excited and continued the process for about three days. I was always careful to replace the horn in its original position to eliminate any curiosity of disturbance.

On the fourth day, I read the trumpet guide, which was next to the tenor horn and followed the directions on how to fold and positioned the lips to create an embouchure. The book clearly explained that this would allow the production of a note. I also studied from the same book, how to play the C Major Scale. In about an hour, I was able to play the first four notes of the C Major Scale. The other four seemed rather high and were quite challenging to produce. In addition, there was some tingling in my lips that did not assure me that I was following the right process. I did not give up. I went back to it again about an hour after, since the tingling had subsided. To my amazement, I was able to play the entire C Major Scale with minimum challenge.

While there was some degree of elation, I now had to figure out how to break the good news to my mother. I knew that the horn would soon be returned to church, so I got in as much practice as possible. One problem though, I could not compose myself. As soon as my mother got home from work in the evening, I approached her and said to her that I wanted her to hear something. I also begged her not to be angry with me. She looked at me with the facial expression, "what has he done wrong now?"

She followed me into the living room as I reached out and took up the trumpet. She looked at me with an even stranger facial expression and asked, "What are you doing?" I replied that I could play the C Major Scale. I played the entire scale. She looked at me in astonishment and asked,…"Who taught you how to play that?" I responded that I taught myself. She seemed to be caught between happy and annoyed. She immediately took up the telephone and called my father at his workplace. I could still remember her exact words: "Ken, this son of yours could play the C Major Scale; apparently he taught himself." I could not hear what the response was from my father's end. However, she hang up the phone and with a smile on her face said, in an authoritative Bajan tone of voice, "I thought I tell you don't touch the people instruments!" I apologized with a bit of charm in my eyes and she immediately walked away.

Weeks later, I was invited to play the kettledrum, instead of a brass instrument, sighting that I could get a hernia at such a young age – 9 years old, from straining to play a wind instrument. My mother thought that it would probably be safer when I was at least one year older. I guess at the time it would not have been common knowledge that children do learn to play instruments at an early age in developed countries. I nevertheless continued to practice on whichever instrument that was brought home. Eventually, I started to gravitate towards the cornet, and in a few months I was asked if I wanted to try reading the 2$^{nd}$ cornet parts at band practice until I can figure out the reading process. This is exactly what I did and the rest is history.

What sensitized me to music from around 8 years old though was my mother allowing me sit next to her in the Salvation Army Band, rather than in the congregation, so that she can keep an eye on my any trace of mischievous behavior.

But even before the cornet days, I had my eyes on the kettledrum. My little break came around the age of 11, when the kettledrum player, Marson Holder, did not show up, and I volunteered to at least keep timing. It did not turn out badly, so I continued to fill in for the kettledrum player any time he was absent. Within a few months, I ended up becoming the second official kettledrum player. The appropriate band uniform was designed for my small frame, a hat slightly oversized, and I became the center of attraction – especially on outdoor gatherings and parades. My goal now was to be one of the official trumpet players in the band.

One day my father surprisingly suggested to my mother that I officially attend band rehearsals and try to learn as much as I can. I sat in the trumpet section and struggled a bit on the 3rd trumpet part. The other players gave me tremendous support. As I improved on the trumpet, I was soon playing lead trumpet in the church band on Sunday mornings and evenings. Eventually, I took music lessons from my father, with a little help from my brother and mother. This served me well as a natural progression into the Royal Barbados Police Force Band as a Band Cadet/Apprentice.

# Chapter 2

## THE ROYAL BARBADOS POLICE FORCE BAND

I joined the Royal Barbados Police Band on May 15, 1972 as Band Apprentice BA, 17 Brathwaite. Christopher Atherley, now Dr. Atherley, was a phenomenal clarinet and tuba player at the time. He was also the associate director of the Salvation Army Band, who filled in when my father was not available. After observing my progress for a while, he suggested that I apply to the Police Band. He advised that I do it before the age of 15, because beyond that age it would be highly unlikely to gain acceptance. I had seen the band perform on parade on a few occasions but had very little information or knowledge on the procedure of becoming a member. As a matter of fact, had it not been for Dr. Atherley, I would probably not have given it any thought at all. The

Police Band Barracks was located at the time at Passage Road, in the city, close proximity to where I lived, yet I was totally oblivious.

I remember, quite vividly, while at Secondary School, writing the application – edited by Dr. Atherley, to the Commissioner of Police at the tender age of 14. I did not anticipate a reply and literally forgot all about it. My parents were not even aware that I had done so.

Many months later, while relaxing at home after school, a police car pulled up in front of my house. A tall, serious looking police officer stepped out of the car and knocked on our little chattel house. I immediately took off to my bedroom, even though I did not recall engaging in any mischievous activities. My mother asked me quite calmly, “Wyckie, did you do something wrong?” I was terrified. My mother politely asked the officer, while gesticulating to me with her hand behind her back, to stand back. My mother, in a warm toned voice, asked, “Can I help you officer?” The officer replied, “Do you have a Wycliffe Brathwaite here?” She hesitantly replied, “Yes Sir.” The officer responded: “Tell him to get dressed; we are here to take him to the Police Band Barracks. Let him pack a small suitcase.” My mother looked bewildered. I immediately rushed back to the living room explaining to my mother that I had applied to be a Police Band Cadet a while ago, forgot to mention it, and did not expect a reply.

The two police officers waited quite patiently in the police car for about 20 minutes until I was dressed. Meanwhile, the curious, closely-knit and densely populated community quickly gathered to get a closer look at what seemed, at a quick glance, to be an arrest. Even, as I was boarding the police car one could hear the whispers and speculations on why I may have been arrested. In fact, as the car drove off some persons were running and peering through the rear car window to get a closer look at the 'potential criminal'.

On arriving to the Police Band Barracks at District "A" Police Station, there were 16 other cadets with gloomy faces. We were briefed that the barracks would be our new home and school for the next year or so. Some of us were openly shaking and crying. Living away from our homes, parents and friends, was surely not what we initially anticipated. We were told that the weekends were ours, while the rest of the week was that of the Police Force.

## Life as a Police Band Cadet

A monthly stipend of BDS $85 to have Mathematics and English teachers come in to teach us, while learning to play an instrument, seemed rather reasonable from my end.

I bought myself a bicycle with my first payment, which I named "Dino" – a popular character from the popular television cartoon "Flintstones". Interestingly, 'Dino" also became my nickname within the Police Band environment, and even beyond.

The 17 new cadets settled in quite nicely -- at least so we all thought. However, there were strange rumors from senior cadets and constables of 'slugging' new cadets within the first three months as some form of indoctrination. Slugging was another term for flogging. This was administered with the multicolored chord that is affixed to the front of the white Police Band tunic.

The Police Band Barracks and District 'A' Police Station, which also housed a branch of the mounted police, were in close proximity. For easy facilitation, there were special garbage cans positioned around the compound where the horses' dung was temporarily dumped.

Unexpectedly, one early morning I was awoken by a bright light shining in my eyes and a slugging/flogging that was too hot to endure. With little hesitation, I flipped out of my sleeping cot, jumped through a nearby window and hit off, as in the sea, into one of the garbage cans with all the horse dung, as my shortest and safest point of refuge. At that point, I did not recall smelling anything out of the ordinary. I was too scared. Meanwhile, I could hear footsteps and unrecognizable voices asking, "Where could he have gone so fast?" I was deep down in the horses' shit, trembling and hoping they did not find me. I overheard one voice shout: "I hope he isn't stupid enough to be hiding in one of those cans with that bad smelling horse shit!" Another voice quickly interjected saying, "Nah. forget him man! Let us check out the other cadets in barrack room number 3." I breathed a sigh of relief, but stayed there for a few minutes longer, in case they were trying to trick me by luring me out of my hiding place. They eventually left the compound, and I made good my escape and took a very long shower. Of course, I returned similar sentiments to a few cadets joining the Band about a year after me.

The Police Band, in my opinion, was an institution of musical excellence. In fact, the band then, under the direction of Senior Superintendent Prince Cave was parallel to any other military band, anywhere else on the planet. There were two trumpet players that I aspired to emulate: the then Station Sargent Herbert Walker and Constable Aaron Thomas, who played 1st and 2nd trumpets respectively. Inspector Gordon Lovell, I found out after one year in the band, was also an excellent trumpet player, but had not played for years due to his administrative duties.

## Arrival of New Long-Model Cornets

I was advised by one of the bandsmen that the band had received about four brand new long-model cornets. I knew they would automatically go to the senior players. I therefore thought I would agitate in the early to be assigned the old one that Aaron Thomas played. I walked presumptuously over to Inspector Lovell's office, without an escort, stood to attention and asked Inspector Lovell if I could be assigned a newer long-model cornet. Protocol in the band is that a junior rank must be escorted by a senior rank in order to approach a high-ranking officer. Inspector Lovell immediately questioned the breach in protocol, but allowed me to stand at ease and state my case. I showed him my short-model cornet with the supported elastic band around the leaking water key, which was causing some stomach discomfort. I presented what I thought was a great case to be assigned a newer or new long-model cornet.

Inspector Lovell took the cornet from me, physically examined it and under his breath whispered…"I haven't touched these things for years, man." He put my battered cornet to his lips and rattled through a few technical exercises. I stood there in amazement and awe at the level of his playing. I thought wow!! He has not played for years? Maybe I should consider stop playing the cornet or switching to another instrument. He slowly gave it back to me with a slight smile on his face and quipped "Nothing is wrong with the horn man! It just needs playing." Saying that I was embarrassed would be an understatement. I was clear in my mind though, that Inspector Gordon Lovell had to be one of my trumpet teachers, at some point, in my Police Band career.

A couple of months after, both Inspector Lovell and Sergeant Walker, at different times, requested that I find a 'trumpet tutor' and meet them in the practice room. Both taught me how to improve my playing by applying different exercises, and how to double and triple-tongue. One thing that stood out when being taught by Station Sargent Walker was the fact that he had very little patience. Once he got over excited, his voice began to shake and he stammered. His words took a bit longer to come out of his mouth than normal. Therefore, if he told you to play a particular exercise and you made too many repeated mistakes, once he began to stammer, this meant that it would be followed by a slap around the head or a strike with whatever object was nearby at the time. Sargent Walker played Lead Trumpet in the main band of about 50 members, inclusive of about six cornet/trumpet players.

Inspector Walker, after a few lessons indicated to me that I am ready to play in the main band. Excited was another understatement.

To be playing with the main band of geniuses was an honor for me and as I was told -- a rare opportunity.

## Change of Instrument?

Another memory that has definitely stayed with me from the tender age of 16 to the present is when Corporal Moore came over to my barrack room and asked, “Where is Dino?” I thought to myself, I do not remember engaging in any mischief of late. Other cadets pointed out that I was in the upper barrack room. I responded: “I am here Sir.” The Corporal approached me suggesting that I show him my fingers. Not knowing for what reason I was doing it, I immediate lengthened my hands showing my fingers. Corporal Moore’s immediate response, with a slight smile on his face: ...“Brathwaite, you have the perfect fingers for either the bassoon or saxophone. Without hesitation, I responded, “Sir, I am not interested in neither the bassoon nor saxophone.” With an authoritative growl, the Corporal retorted, “Brathwaite, you don’t decide what instrument you will play in the Band. You are assigned to the instrument that we believe you would excel on.” I argued that I like the trumpet, and this is the reason why I joined the band in the first place, having been on the trumpet for over one year. This back and forth continued for about two minutes, before Corporal Moore stormed off suggesting that he would begin to put this in effect shortly.

## Protest

I was so devastated that I decided it must be dealt with at a higher level before it was too late. I marched myself, again, directly to Inspector Gordon Lovell's office in hope that I could counter this nuisance.

As earlier mentioned, protocol within the Police Band dictates that in order to approach a high-ranking officer such as an Inspector, it must be facilitated by a rank just below that of Inspector – Station Sergeant. Out of disgust, I broke that protocol. I approached Inspector Lovell's office and knocked on his office door. The inspector's voice rang out with "come in." I must admit that at that point I became very nervous and knew that there was no way I could back out of this now.

I opened the door, marched smartly up to the Inspector's desk, came to attention, saluted with style and said, "Good morning Sir." Inspector Lovell immediately glanced around with a bewildered look on his face and asked "Did you come here alone without being escorted Brathwaite?" I responded, "Yes Sir. May I stand at ease and explain myself Sir?" He may have forgotten that this was not the first time I broke the protocol. Anyway, my request was granted. I then explained to him that Corporal Moore is suggesting that I switch from trumpet to another instrument, and I love the trumpet. I also explained that should I have to switch I would have no choice but to resign from the band. After a few minutes in trying to understand Corporal Moore's rationale for wanting me to switch from trumpet, he angrily ordered me to summon Corporal Moore to his office and to return as well. This too was outside of the normal protocol.

Both Corporal Moore and I walked back to the Inspector's office – Corporal Moore slightly ahead of me. I quietly observed Corporal Moore trying nervously to convince Inspector Lovell that there was a shortage of saxophone players and a dire need for a bassoon player. He argued that I was chosen because of my potential. Corporal Moore also suggested that he gave me a choice of one or the other. I could see the anger on Inspector Lovell's face. By this time, I started to feel a sense of regret. I felt like I may have created an unnecessary problem. However, right in front of me – a mere band cadet -- Inspector Lovell made it clear that no one should be forced to play an instrument they did not like. He then ordered Corporal Moore to let me remain on trumpet and there would be no further discussion on the matter. Inspector Lovell then literally 'barked'...attention!! Both Corporal Moore and I came to attention. We were then dismissed and we marched out of the office together and went our separate ways without looking at each other or engaging in any further dialogue.

Although there was no further dialogue on the matter, there was continued tension between Corporal Moore and me for months after. There were times that I came on parade or to cadet rehearsal late and there was absolutely no acknowledgement. This was probably just as painful as having to switch to another instrument. It was as though I had been relegated to the status of visitor and not a legitimate member of the Royal Barbados Police Band.

## Engagement Money

The Police Band, in addition to the regular salary, also received extra funds from paid engagements. These funds were referred to as 'engagement money'. It was disbursed on a quarterly basis, generally after six months performance with the big band.

After about eight months of playing engagements with the main band, I still had not received any engagement funds. I queried it with some of the senior constables and it was unanimous that I might have been inadvertently overlooked. I was advised that there was a particular day when those funds were disbursed and on that day I should politely go up to Station Sargent Herbert Walker's office and just ask a question. The way Sargent Walker's office was situated one could see if he is in his office from glancing up from the ground level to his office upstairs.

I looked up stairs and realized that Sgt. Walker was in his office. I proceeded up the long flight of stairs and lightly knocked on his door. There was no response. I knew he was there, so I knocked again. There was still no answer. After a few more knocks there was a harsh voice-tone of … "come in." I opened the door, walked in, came to attention and greeted him as "Good morning Sir." There was no response, not even recognition of me being there. I realized there was a lot of money on his desk and he seemed to be focused on counting it or parceling it out. After standing at attention and waiting for at least three minutes for a response, he eventually looked up over his glasses and asked abruptly with a stammer "Wha… wha… what you want Brathwaite?" I responded in a soft and respectful voice: "Sorry to disturb you Sir, but I have been playing out with the main band for more than six months now and just wanted to find out if I was entitled to engagement money as yet?"

Without delay, Sargent Walker pushed all the money from his desk onto the ground and shouted again with a stammer, and in raw Bajan dialect: "blima... blima...look it all there! tek um up." I stood there speechless and frozen, with the dilemma of ambivalence of two possible options - should I apologize, come to attention and exit the office or should I pick up the scattered money and place it back on his desk? I decided the most respectful thing to do would be to pick up the money, apologize for the trouble and make a quick exit.

As I bent down to do so, I heard a loud noise of a stick hitting the door behind me, barely missing my head by a few inches and a loud stammering voice shouting, again in raw Bajan dialect: "touch um! touch um!" I explained that I was just going to put it back on his desk to save him the trouble. He ordered me to leave his office at once, if I knew what was good for me. I immediately came to attention and reversed out of his office. I was not going to take any chances of backing him on the way out.

On my way back down the stairs from Station Sargent Walker's office, I could hear loud chuckles from cadets and senior bandsmen. They were all curious of the noise that came from Sgt. Walker's office. As I tried to recreate the events in order as they happened, the crowd got bigger and bigger and the laughter was almost deafening. I was set up. Even as I departed the Police Band in 1974, I had not received any engagement money.

## A Rebellious Band Cadet

I can admit that I did not take too kindly to the notion of coming to attention or saluting when a senior officer passed within my space. Being raised a Christian, this seemed odd to me. It felt like I was worshiping man. Some argued that I had no discipline or did not respect authority. More than 40 years after, it still rubs me the wrong way.

There was a time while walking on the compound behind a senior member - Corporal Moore, when he deliberately dropped the newspaper that was under his arm on the ground. He glanced back, while he continued walking, to see if I would pick it up. I knew that he had dropped it deliberately, so I continued walking as well. Corporal Moore stopped and asked me if I had not seen that the paper dropped out of his hand, and the right thing to do would have been to pick it up. I argued that I was aware that he deliberately dropped the paper expecting me to pick it up and that was not fair. I was eventually reprimanded and locked up in the barracks for a month, as a result. This meant not being able to leave the barracks at any time for a full month, including weekends. My mother had to take the bus every day for the full month to bring me food. It was painful watching the other cadets leave and return to the compound having fun, while I was confined to the boring Police Band Barracks.

On another occasion, the senior cadet, Cheltenham, as a form of punishment, put me in the middle of the barracks yard looking up at the sun. The deputy senior cadet, Boyce, who passed me looking up at the sun, queried why I was looking up at the sun when reading music was part of my job as a Band Apprentice. I explained that I was punished for eating in the library. He immediately commanded me to go out of the sun. The Senior Cadet soon realized that I had moved, gripped me by the collar and walked me back into the sun. The sixteen other junior cadets, with whom I joined the band, came to my rescue forming a circle around the senior cadet and took turns in slapping him around the head as he made several attempts to get out of the circle. What was probably supposed to be a fun event turned out quite differently.

The following morning, all the cadets that were involved, including me, were summoned to the Deputy Director's office. The message sent to all of the cadets was to clean our belts and boots to be shining like 'dog-stones'. Apparently, we were all facing summary dismissal. Corporal Moore, who was in charge of the 17 junior cadets thought this was the opportune time to get back at me and formulated the argument that I was the ringleader; this is without having any details of what actually transpired. It would have been disrespectful to interject. It appeared as though I was targeted and might be the only one in trouble. However, one question from the Deputy Director, to Corporal Moore probably saved me. The question posed by deputy director, Morris to the Corporal was …"Corporal Moore, can he play?" There was a slight hesitation and then a response of "Yes Sir!"

"He is probably the best of the lot Sir." There was even a longer pause and then a directive from the Deputy Director: "Take him and lock him up man! Make sure he doesn't see outside for a while." The others walked away free and I was confined to Barracks for two months. Despite my always getting into trouble, I cherished the two and a half years I would have spent in that institution. It taught me discipline and respect for others.

## Institution of Excellence

The Royal Barbados Police Force Band was the launching pad for my career as a professional musician. It was a place of excellence. During my time in the Band, I had never heard any mistakes during engagements. All the mistakes and fine-tuning were done under the careful watch of Musical Director, Prince Cave during rehearsals.

I used to enjoy one particular March the Band always played on parade – "Colonel Boogie" and a piece which showcased the trumpet section entitled "Buglers' Holiday". These were the first pieces I located in the music library and did not hesitate to practice them until they were as close to perfect as possible. It was always a joy and amazing to hear Buglers' Holiday brilliantly performed by the three top trumpet players in the band then – Sargent Walker, and Constables Aaron Thomas and 'Fobbie' Johnson. The double and triple-tonguing techniques required to execute the piece was simply flawless. I would always tell myself I must be able to play like that.

In one year. I was playing at a very high level and playing very technical pieces at the very back of the Arban trumpet tutor.

## Promotion

The Police Band seemed not to have a strategic developmental plan for young cadets who had excelled beyond average performance. My playing excelled in the Police Band very rapidly. I was constantly told how good I was and this was verbalized so frequently that I became more and more frustrated with the system. Musical pieces frequently played by the band were no longer challenging, and being promoted to the first, second, or even third trumpet stands seemed rather farfetched.

Questions about acceleration promotion surfaced from time to time, since the stipulated earliest age to be promoted to constable was 18. This acceleration promotion was supposed to allow young talented band members who were ineligible for promotion the opportunity to receive the same pay as constables. The promotion system was a critical issue. So critical, that some band constables sought promotion by transferring to the patrol division of the police force and returned later to the band after gaining promotion. The Police Band was allotted a certain number of senior and constable ranks, and that was written in stone. It seems as though there was no choice for me, then, other than to pursue external bands to earn extra funds. In fact, I did not have to go in search of such. Most poplar bands actually pursued me instead.

# Chapter 3

## BANDS EXPERIENCE

### The Music Circle

While still being a cadet of the police band, at age 16, I was engaged in band rehearsals and performances with an all-teenage pop band called The Music Circle. The band comprised of some of the most dynamic young musicians in the country: Linus Yaw, bass; Ian Gibson, drums; Michael Cheeseman, lead and rhythm guitar; Graham Wilkinson, keyboards; McGregor Leonard on lead vocals and both Jeffrey Grannum and myself - cadets in the Police Band, on sax and trumpet respectively. Below is a photo of four of the original musicians of the The Music Circle: Jeff Gannum to the far left, to the right of him, Michael Cheeseman, Ricky Brathwaite in the middle and the late David Hooper, the band manager, to the far right.

As a matter of fact, most of the musicians from that era are today still known and a few have gone on to great musical horizons.

So dynamic was the 1973/1974 band Music Circle, that the band became the talk of the town. We played with the more established bands of the times, such as The Outfit, and The Blue Rhythm Combo (BRC). One could tell from the facial expressions of the more established band members the respect for the young boys on the block. Actually, it was these band encounters that laid the path for the pursuit of saxophonist, Jeffrey Grannum and myself by the most dynamic band of the time, The Outfit. Other popular bands such as The Checkmates and Wendy Alleyne and the Dynamics had also contacted me about joining their bands; but I felt that even though those bands were popular, they lacked musicality and musicianship. The Outfit, BRC and Troubadours International were the bands to which I frequently listened. Police Band Cadets – horn players - would frequent where BRC and Troubadours were playing. The BRC's horn section was dynamic. Trinidadian trumpeter, Kirk Dalaway was always the talk of the town, because of the high notes he could play with little effort. Comparing him with Vincentian trumpet player, Raymond "Alfie" Blake of The Troubadours International would always be the discussion of the day. Raymond Blake was not known for high notes, but for his clean execution and trumpet technique. In fact, The Troubadours International horn section of Prince Cave Jr, Raymond “Alfie” Blake and Trevor “Baje” Walcott sounded smooth, balanced and like a digital recording in an analogue world.

Interestingly, the late David Hooper, the band manager and trombone player in the photo bought a trombone and decided he would join the horn section. He turned up on a gig one night, without any knowledge of the trombone or without any prior rehearsal and proceeded to play in the horn section. This raised many red flags, because Hooper managed to get the correct notes on any position. This was nothing short of amazing or genius. Because of his onstage showmanship, he actually attracted curious onlookers, who thought he was legitimate, and probably the best player in the section. Playing simultaneously with the Police Band and the Music Circle opened new possibilities for me as a professional performer and touring musician.

## The Outfit

While still a member of both the Police and Music Circle bands, I was contacted by the late, Franklyn Greaves, the manager of The Outfit. He convinced me that the band was about to engage in great things and this would require me resigning from both the Police Band and The Music Circle and committing totally to The Outfit.

*The 1974 Bajan Band, The Outfit, in Rivière-du-Loup, Quebec, Canada.*

I was convinced that The Outfit was a great move and I resigned from The Music Circle, but remained in the Police Band.

I was the youngest member of the band at age 16. Other members included in the above photo are, from left (bottom): the late, Bertie Connell, guitar and lead vocals; the late, Ricky Aimey, (bandleader), bassist and lead vocalist; the late, Hayden Hinds/Bells, lead vocals and percussion and O'brien Thomas, saxophone and lead vocal. From left, top: Brian Walker, keyboards; Wayne Walcott, trombone; Chess Haynes, lead vocals; Ricky Brathwaite, trumpet/flugelhorn; and the late, Randolph Lavine on drums.

After months of playing with such amazing musicians, I finally began to learn how to improvise on my instrument. This is something I thought was missing from the Police Band, as it was in my opinion too classically centered. The band manager tapped into this area of my life when he suggested to my mother and me that I would do much better musically, if I resigned from the Police Band and go professional. He tried to convince me that I was very talented and the Police Band might be a dead end.

I further discussed this with my mother, who ended up confusing me. Her argument was that the Police Band was a real job; there was the collection of pension at age 65, and she gave many other reasons why I should not leave certain for uncertain. She did subsequently reason with me though explaining that I made the decision to join the band and she would support whatever choice I made. I decided to tender my resignation, with one month's notice.

I recall arriving home one afternoon for lunch, during the process of my resignation, and finding Corporal Moore in conversation with my mother in the living room. I did not know the nature of the conversation, because I politely acknowledged his presence and went back to the barracks without having my lunch. When I arrived home in the evening, my mother summoned me to her bedroom and told me Corporal Moore unexpectedly showed up and tried to convince her that I was making a colossal mistake in resigning and that she should dissuade me, because he could see me one day as Musical Director of the Police Band. My mother echoed the same sentiments. She had no influence in my joining the institution and therefore had no influence in my decision to quit.

I ended up departing the Police Band, but it surely was not a natural progression. Migrating to the external band life brought a different set of issues - tardiness, indiscipline, musical mistakes, excessive swearing, and marijuana smoking among others.

I remember the drummer in The Outfit, the late, Randolph "Ranny" Lavine, reprimanding me for continually looking back when someone made a mistake. He forcefully indicated that the next time I engaged in this unprofessional habit of looking around when there was a mistake, he would embarrass me in public, and he did.

One night while performing for a show in the Flambeau Bar of the prestigious Hilton Hotel in Barbados, the drummer, during a funk song, executed a drum break and landed slightly behind the beat, slightly throwing off the rhythm. As soon as I looked back, the drummer got off the drums, walked calmly over to the horn section at the front of the stage, struck me with his pair of drumsticks on my right shoulder and quipped …"I warned you about looking back!" I was extremely embarrassed, because when I glanced into the audience of about 300 persons, I observed laughter coming from some persons siting in the front row. I am not sure if they believed it to be a part of the show. This was a learning curve, because I kept playing with my head forward for the remainder of the night. I cannot recall ever looking around again when there was a mistake.

This experience of not looking around once things did not go according to plan compounded by the lash across my shoulder all served me well as part of the developmental process in not allowing the audience to recognize if there is a mistake. This is a great lesson for younger musicians and persons within the Performing Arts. Even with the confrontation between the drummer, Ranny Lavine and myself, we both migrated to Canada in the same band, and became very close friends.

# Chapter 4

## Province De Québec, Here I Come

Chez Haynes, one of the lead vocalists in the band, arranged a 3-month tour for The Outfit to French Canada when I was 17 years old. The tour was a short one and was a painful journey. There was no mummy to cook for me, wash my clothes or to talk with if I had an issue. I also cried having to leave my 16-year-old girlfriend, Sandra Walton, who I had only met three months prior.

The 3-months stint turned out to be 3 years instead. Most of the other members of the band knew that the contract to Canada was more than a 3-month stint, but thought telling me the truth would have hindered any chance of me going on the tour in the first place, and they were absolutely correct. However, after six months of playing all over Canada and meeting new friends, I became so comfortable that the only person I actually missed back home was my mother.

Our arrival in French Canada, The Province du Québec was a cultural shock for most members of the band. First, no one briefed us on the temperature in Canada and that it would be freezing. Most of us were wearing handmade six-inch "clogs" - platform shoes with the toes out. We did not have the appropriate winter clothing, only light sweaters.

As the plane drew nearer and nearer to Canada, before even landing, there was some indication of how cold it was on the ground. In fact, one of the band members joked asking if someone had opened the deepfreeze on the plane, to loud laughter. When the plane landed and we disembarked, we were not the only ones laughing. We instantly became the laughing stock of the town. We were sliding every two to three steps on the snow and ice on the ground. We made light of the experience by actually laughing at each other as well. No member of the band spoke French and no member of the Québécois public spoke English. There were also no other black faces around but those of the band. It was a real culture shock because we felt like aliens from out of space. Actually, one year after, now speaking and understanding Quebecois [Canadian French], a young boy around 6 years old gesticulated to his mother: "Momie regarde un singe." The English translation is Mummy look there is a monkey.

There was another occasion that shocked the band members. Our agent dispatched us to perform in a small town called Chicoutimi. We arrived at the hotel where we would stay and play for the month. People at the hotel were staring at us as though we were aliens. A Caucasian man, probably in his 40s, requested to rub the bass player's hand. He wanted to satisfy himself that we were in fact black and not painted. The members of the band were amazed at the ignorance, but at that time the people of Chicoutimi, one of the first towns we toured, had never seen black people in person, only on television.

The band Outfit toured the Province du Québec for three straight years. We drove miles on miles from hotel to hotel in a large bus with a trailer full of equipment that was assigned to us by the agency. We played at least 25 times per month to packed lounges and nightclubs for the entire three-year period. The first thing that we investigated on arrival to any hotel was if there was a nice big, high stage. There were times when we were disappointed, but we made up for it in performances.

Some hotels presented a challenge where rehearsals for the band were not practical. The band could not practice new songs, because of the proximity of the stage to the bar. The bar generated customers who bought drinks during the course of day well into the night, especially if they thought that there might be a large crowd preventing them from gaining entry to the night session. The band, therefore, had to work out an unusual system of learning new songs. There were jukeboxes located at most hotels. One would insert a Canadian quarter and select the desired song. It took quite a few quarters before all the horn, bass, keyboard and vocal parts could be retained. The band would then perform the song on the night with few mistakes. In about two performances, the song would be played with hardly any mistakes. This system developed a form of air training for the band members to the point where most members could actually identify the key of a song; recognize the various notes to the song, including various patterns, without reference to an instrument.

## "Trouble Does Not Set Up Like Rain"

My mother would frequently recite to me as a young boy: ... "Trouble does not set up like rain." – In other words, there is never a rainbow that would indicate the likeliness of trouble.

One of the reasons why we had to develop this system of practice was due to a fracas that almost got us into deep trouble. At one point, in a small hotel in the small French town of Alma, the band thought it could try to get in a short practice on the stage during the lunch period. Again, the stage and bar areas were in close approximation to each other. There was always some form of activity at the bar, but the arrangement was to rehearse only with the selective instruments: bass, guitar, keyboards – the instruments that can be controlled by volume knobs. The other members would be there, but only to observe, and to avoid any high volume issues.

Twenty minutes into the experimental arrangement the bass player queried why the power went off on his bass amplifier. Shortly after, both the keyboard and guitar players reported that the power had gone off on their amplifiers as well. It was quickly realized that either the electricity had gone off or the breaker tripped. I was observing the rehearsal from the comfort of a stool by the bar. I immediately asked the person serving the drinks behind the bar, who happened to be the owner's daughter, if she could check to see if the breaker had tripped. She did not answer, even though I would have asked nicely, more than once. At this point, I could hear the players on the stage shouting that she – the owner's daughter had cut the power supply to the stage. The drummer angrily began to do a loud solo performance on the drums. He shouted, "Turn offs these now!" I found the whole affair very jovial so I started to laugh. At that point, I felt the coldest water ever thrown in my face. The owner's daughter threw extremely cold water in my face, while an older Caucasian man sitting at the bar punched me on my forehead. Initially, I was confused and thought about not retaliating for fear of being deported, but on second thought, could not resist the temptation.

I ended up fighting with the man who punched me, while the entire band tried desperately to get me off of him. My position was, what did I do? After all heads had calmed down, I headed upstairs to my room and decided to get a shower.

## Police Custody

While in the shower, which was located in a cul-de-sac down the hallway of the hotel, I heard a knocking on the bathroom door. The police identified themselves and asked if I could meet them downstairs after showering. They were very polite. I responded in French, that I would be down in less than five minutes.

As promised, I headed downstairs and three police officers in uniform greeted me. I was a bit confused to see the hotel owner's daughter lying on the floor in front of the bar holding her back and weeping loudly. This incident had happened approximately forty-five minutes earlier. The police explained to me that the owner's daughter had made a call to the station reporting that a black musician had wounded her on the back with a drinking glass and she was bleeding. I did notice blood on her hands and thought, well…I am definitely in trouble. I may even be deported for injuring a female. I knew I did not do it, but decided to remain quiet and just observe.

The police requested, quite gently, that I accompany them to the police station to fill out a report. They opened the backdoor of the police car – the professional way, ensuring that my head did not hit the top of the car door.

I noticed when we got to the station that the officers were clowning around and having fun. It did not appear as though they were overly concerned with me being present. After about a fifteen-minute wait, one officer finally introduced himself to me and proceeded to question me about the incident. I did so in French, which I spoke fluently at the time. I could tell the police officer either liked me or was very caring. At the end of my statement, he softly said, "I believe you." He explained that the police have had several issues in the past with the owner's daughter and her husband. He said very politely, that he would have the police officers take me back to the hotel. He, however, cautioned me that I should expect trouble, because her husband was released from prison only a week ago. I communicated this to the other band members, but gave it very little attention.

## Interrupted Performance

One week later, when we had forgotten all about the episode, four buffed looking, bodybuilder-type men, walked in front of the stage during a performance, looked up angrily towards me on the stage and shouted in French, “arrêter la musique” (Stop the music). We continued playing, but one of the three men wanted to establish that this was not a joke, so decided to pull the microphone stand from in front of the trombone player down to the dance floor. By then, the owner of the hotel appeared out of nowhere and tried to persuade them to leave. We observed one of the men tossing the owner away like a ragdoll. We recognized there was a serious situation developing, so we stopped playing and armed ourselves with microphone stands and any blunt object we could find.

The men were frowned upon by the audience present -- some on the dance floor, and others seated. The audience’s support allowed the owner to forcefully convince them to refrain from causing trouble and leave the hotel. We took a short break and resumed playing but with some degree of caution. Apparently, the men decided to leave the hotel. After the performance, we retired immediately to one of the band member’s room. We did not think that it had ended so easily and peacefully. We thought that the men might be up to no good. Amazingly, they had actually left the compound.

## A Husband’s Rage

Days had passed when I was in the shower again. This time, it was not the police, but the owner asking if I could come to a particular room when I was finished showering just to have a brief chat. I agreed. As soon as I came out of the shower clad only in a towel, I was grabbed by a muscular man who pushed me into a room near to the bathroom. He pushed me down on the bed and started shouting in French: "You are a dead man. How could you hit my wife?" At this time, the owner was pleading with the man saying, "You promised me you only wanted to talk to him." I tried not to agitate him any further, because he was huge and angry. I tried to explain to him that his wife was not truthful, and that I had never hit a female in my life. Maybe the noise and shouting alerted Wayne Walcott, the trombone player in the band. Wayne, a Trinidadian and over six feet tall was generally quiet, until he got upset.

I recall Wayne knocking on the room door like a man possessed, asking, "Rick are you ok?" I replied yes. He continued, "You sure?" Before I could respond again, there was a loud noise and the entire room door came crashing to the ground. It was like a professional football player tackling another player, or a bulldozer ramming down the door. Wayne charged in, grabbed the man by his throat, raising him slightly off the ground. I begged and begged Wayne to stop and let the man go, that I was ok. Wayne however repeatedly suggested to the man to pick on people his own size. The owner at this time had his head clasped between both hands and weeping uncontrollably. The man began to apologize while Wayne walked him out of the room by the scruff of his neck and shouted at him to leave now, which he did without hesitation. What was supposed to be a month's stay and performance at the hotel was abruptly curtailed. The agent called and explained that another hotel about 300 miles away wanted the band, and we should leave right away in order to get there in good time. We left discussing while pondering on that true popular Bajan proverb: "Trouble does not set up like rain".

## A Missed Opportunity

One year the band was given the opportunity to play on a televised show in Montreal: a show that could possibly propel us to the big times. This was a welcomed opportunity, since we had grown accustomed to the smaller French Canadian cities and not the customary popular metropolitan areas.

We drove for about 7 hours from the town called Alma all the way to Montreal to meet and finalize details on this special gig. Of course, cellular phones were not yet invented, so when we arrived in Montreal we were told that arrangements were made to have another group perform, because there was no communication from our agent and the group could not be located on the road. We explained that we were driving for hours, hungry, in need of a bath, had no funds; but all we got was an apology.

## Out in the Cold

It was a nightmare. Nine members, black men too, walked around the city of Montreal wondering where we were going to stay for the night, and what we were going to eat. We mustered enough courage to approach a small motel-hotel and convinced the owner that we drove all the way from Alma for a gig that fell through and if it were remotely possible to stay there until we found another gig. We promised her that we would pay her more than the going rate once we found another gig. She agreed, but indicated that she could not provide meals as well. We appreciated just the room and board, because it was freezing outside. A whole week passed without food or money to buy food. I had $20 in my pocket, which I used to buy an Oh Henry [chocolate] and a small coke. I ensured that this 'meal' lasted me an entire week. Some band members had similar amounts, while others had no money at all. Members slept as long as possible during the night and woke up as late as possible in the day so that the interval between morning and night would be as short as possible - little time to think about food.

## The Blues Busters: Jamaican Reggae Duo

One evening while the full band gathered in the percussionist/lead vocalist, Hayden Bells' room to plan what the next move would be, the owner of the hotel knocked on the door and said there were two men to see us. It was the Jamaican reggae duo, "The Blues Busters". I had heard of this popular singing group from a child. They said to us that they heard that there was a great musical group from Barbados in town and they wanted to talk business. Our eyes lit up almost in harmony. Someone knew that the band was in town? We invited them into one of our bedrooms and listened to what they were offering. They asked us if we would be willing to back them in a show at the prestigious downtown Edgewater Hotel. We agreed, but explained that we had not eaten food in days. They assured us that there was a restaurant located within the Edge water Hotel and they would organize dinner for us, either before or after the concert.

There was no way of getting in a rehearsal, so we convinced them that we had developed a system for learning songs over the years that would work well at this time. They appeared to trust us, so we listened carefully to the approximately ten songs they wanted to perform. Of course, we also had to assure them that we would do everything to make the show a success.

## Show Time

The show, which took place two days after, was well executed with unrehearsed dance moves and a tight musical performance. Patrons were extremely happy. The Blues Busters were so happy that they joked around after the show suggesting we might want to consider not eating at least two weeks before a concert. We were invited to the restaurant after the concert where a sumptuous buffet was already set up for all the artists on the show. We were also paid in cash, an amount exceeding our expectations.

The first thing on our agenda was to repay the hotel owner who was so gracious in allowing us to stay at her hotel-motel without any hustles. The actual amount eludes me now, but I am certain the hotel owner received double what the average charge would have been. I can remember, quite vividly, that she was very grateful. She allowed us to make a long distance call to our agent, without charge. The agent was annoyed at the whole charade, but rebooked us at another hotel in a town only a few miles away. He made sure that we could get there on the few dollars left over and eventually refunded us for the gas, meals, hotel cost and any other expenditure endured during the ordeal.

## Lac-Mégantic

There were other strange occurrences while touring the Provence De Quebec. Another small town called Lac-Mégantic is also etched in my mind. The band could always tell on visiting a town if we would be welcomed and celebrated or merely tolerated.

The first day we arrived at our hotel in Lac-Mégantic we did not like the stage or the way we were treated. This sentiment manifested itself when we all descended to the restaurant for our lunch. We did not get the opportunity to ask what was for lunch. The waitress approached the table I was sitting at with four other band members and placed the first plate on the table. It contained beans. We anticipated a good meal. Then we realized that other plates with beans were also placed on the other tables where the other band members were sitting.

We sat waiting for about 20 minutes to see what other dishes would accompany the beans. We could see the waitress sitting in the far corner of the restaurant looking quite melancholy. After a while, a member of the band decided to motion to the waitress to approach our table. No one spoke English in this town. The guitarist, Bertie Connell, asked in French, what were we having with the beans. The waitress replied, “beans et beans.” This translates in English: beans and beans. Some members laughed openly, and others showed their disgust by getting up from the table and going back to their rooms. We found out that there was a nearby pizzeria, which facilitated call-in orders. Our contracts always stipulated the inclusion of meals, but we were too hungry for any level of negotiation at that point.

However, we made an urgent call to the agent explaining and making it abundantly clear that we were not standing for this scant respect and were not interested in any more performances at this hotel. The agent indicated that he would make a few calls and get back to us within the hour. He did, with good news of moving to another hotel gig about three hours away. We packed up and left without saying goodbye. I vividly remember a band member, in utter disgust, punching a hole in his bedroom wall on his way out to the lobby, where we would wait for departure transportation.

## Home Away From Home

Canada was undeniably my second home, because it was the first metropolitan space I had visited at the tender age of 17. The first thing I wanted to do once I got to Canada was to play and frolic in the snow. This is something of which I had always dreamed. The photo shows me at age 17 standing in the snow with unbuttoned shirt. This was met with nebulous facial expressions from the community as to say… 'He must be crazy'. The possibility of attracting some form of illness was one of the concerns. I still believe the rays from sun were still present in my small frame; because even though the temperature was below zero, this had very little effect on my body.

I particularly enjoyed the friendships I had developed with my white French girlfriends as I moved from city to city, town to town. They were mostly very naive, because we were all of tender ages and we all struggled to understand each other culturally. This helped them to learn English, while I soon began to speak Fluent French. Their parents did not show any signs of racism towards me.

Anna in photo at left and Lisa in photo at right were special friends, because their parents treated me like their son. Lisa Gagnon's parents had bought a beach house by the lake and this was home for her family and me in the summer. Boat rides, fishing and exercising were some of the enjoyable features: not to mention the varieties of home cooked French foods that Lisa's mother enjoyed preparing on a daily basis.

She would ensure that I ate all of my food. I was not prepared to give up this luxury, but fate would have it differently.

Most members of The Outfit really enjoyed Canada, to the point that we had made it our home for three years. We all had white girlfriends and spent time with them in different cities, at their apartments or with their families when we were off from gigs. One of my girlfriends, Linda Faucher, who was four years older than me, was so obsessed with the relationship that she insisted that we dressed alike – scarf and all, as shown in the photo below.

*Ricky and Linda at Linda's: (Alma, Quebec)*

After one year together, Linda and I engaged in several discussions on getting married. I approached it with some degree of ambivalence but called home to Barbados to get a feel for how my mother felt about this bold move at age 18. Linda got the opportunity to speak with my mother via the telephone as well. From the tone of the dialogue and length of the conversation, I could deduce that my mother liked Linda. However, when the phone was handed back to me, my mother asked me two questions, "Ricky, is she black or white? How old is she?" I responded that she was white and about four years older than I was. There was a slight pause, then my mother, in Bajan dialect, opined …"Listen, it is your choice, but you ain't see a star pitch yet…Tek your time." I actually anticipated this response from my mother. On hanging up, I communicated my mother's sentiments to Linda. I witnessed another side to Linda that I had never seen before. She used strong words and metaphors to describe how stupid I was and had no mind of my own. The relationship abruptly came to an end. As a matter of fact, Linda called a taxi and ordered me to leave her apartment immediately. This was around four o'clock in the morning. Luckily, the only thing that I kept at Linda's apartment was a few pieces of clothing and my trumpet.

The taxi came in approximately thirty minutes and took me to the train station. The taxi driver collected his fare and left. I realized only 15 seconds after the taxi parted that the train station was closed. There was no one else in sight, and no house in close proximity. It was about 15 degrees below zero. In order to keep warm, I had to run around the train station in a winter coat, boots, two pairs of socks, no mittens, for approximately two hours until the station superintendent came. He realized instantly on arrival what was going on. He opened the door with some alacrity and invited me to come in. He explained that it would be a while before the heat came on. By this time, I had collapsed on the floor from exhaustion and could barely feel any sensation in my legs. Two or three passengers arrived periodically and assisted me to a bench near to the central heating mechanism. I slowly returned to normal, especially in my legs and the palms of my hands. I never heard of or ran into Linda after that ordeal. I did not want to. It was a very painful occasion that still causes me to cringe whenever I have to relay the story to someone else.

I must admit that Linda's drastic change in her feelings for me, to the point of asking me to leave, left an indelible bad taste in my mouth – a taste that would alter my behavior towards women and marriage in general for many years after. In fact, I may have destroyed a few genuine female relationships as a result. I must admit that because of the closeness between the members of the band and their positive advice after hearing the story, helped tremendously in shaping the negative residue that was beginning to affect my positive relationship with females – black, white, brown or yellow.

## Immigration Hiccup

After three years of residing in French Canada – travelling from state to state, city to city – the band was contacted by the Canadian Immigration Department. We were asked to visit the office, in the near future, to discuss the band's status in Canada. We had no idea what to expect once we visited the immigration department. We contemplated that it would probably be to regularize our Canadian status as residents.

We were advised by friends not to go in, since we were legitimate, as far as work permits were concerned, and had not been involved in anything mischievous. We thought that the right thing to do would be to visit the immigration office, as requested, and respect the law.

On visiting the immigration office we were all escorted to an isolated room in the back. The discussion was centered on the band being eligible for permanent resident status, because of the time that had elapsed working in Canada. We were all elated and welcomed the opportunity: after all, Quebec was the place we had called our home for three years.

In order to legitimize our qualification for permanent residency, and for this to take effect, we were given two options: either to go across the Canadian border or home to Barbados for only a day or two – which ever was the more feasible. Again, our former band manager, Barbadian, Franklyn Greaves warned us that the government was tricking us into breaking the eligibility for residency status by crossing the border. Once this occurred before any paper work was filed, this would disrupt the automatic privilege to residency. We thought we were adhering to the requirements of the law and went against the advice of friends and Franky. We decided to travel to Barbados for what we believed to be a well-deserved home-space for a week of relaxation before the hard work resumes.

The truth is that most members of the band Outfit would continually allude to the notion of never returning to Barbados. They seemed to have been based on the premise that Barbados was a small myopic space that embraced academia and frowned on the Arts and raw talent. Even returning to perform for one night was a taboo. The common consensus on spending a few days in Barbados was there would absolutely be no performance. The common consensus was that the trip would be strictly related to immigration matters.

# Chapter 5

---

## Barbados Uh Come From

We booked our flights to Barbados, leaving most of our clothes, and in some cases, our instruments, back in Canada. In fact, the drummer, Randolph "Ranny" Lavine, hesitantly left his new 12-piece Pearl drum set behind.

News quickly spread around town that the Outfit was in town, and we had several lucrative booking offers in a short space of time. Immigration matters took much longer than anticipated, cash flow began to dwindle and the initial position on performing while in Barbados was forced to change.

## Pieces of Eight Night Club

Our main performance was at the Pieces of Eight Night Club in Hastings, Christ Church, Barbados. To our amazement, the place was completely packed to capacity. The crowd could not get enough renditions by Earth Wind & Fire and other technical songs by other popular American groups such as Chicago, KC and the Sunshine Band, Kool and The Gang, among others. The massive crowd pushed and shouted as though Michael Jackson was performing. Patrons had never witnessed a local band of such high caliber. Actually, we were supposed to share the stage with the band Harmony - one of the more popular local bands in the country at the time. After our performance, Harmony did not want to go on stage. We had to convince them to do what they were known and loved for, rather than try to compete with what had just transpired. They eventually went on stage and were well received. The overwhelming reception, support, love and respect from that first gig opened up many other performing possibilities for The Outfit band. We decided not to perform again, for fear of over exposure, plus we were supposed to be heading back to Canada in about a week or so.

The band was finally summoned to the Canadian Embassy in Barbados. We all held our breaths as we approached the office. Many questions were asked and the trajectory of the questions did not seem favorable. We were asked: "Who suggested that you file official papers in Barbados?" We explained it was the Canadian immigration authorities in Canada. We saw the official held his head between his hands and softly explained that the filing of papers for Canadian status must be done from the Canadian end. The bodies of all members of the band immediately went numb. Essentially, we were told that we could go back to Canada as individuals, but not as a group. This we understood, after the fact, was due to tardiness on the Canadian immigration part failing to monitor the band's performance and work status in Canada over the years. This meant that our eligibility for permanent residency status was no longer possible. The band tried to continue performances in Barbados, but soon became regular and irrelevant. This frustration was the catalyst for the demise of one of the finest bands to emerge on the Barbadian cultural landscape – The Outfit.

## Devastation

The band members were devastated. Most members actually cried. Ranny, one of the finest drummers to grace the Barbadian shores, never recovered from this ordeal and eventually quit playing drums, while turning to heavy alcohol consumption.

I was left with very few options at the time and the Barbados hotel circuit seemed the most feasible. I put together several small groups all of which broke up after short stints. I decided to put together a group that would be versatile enough to play on the hotel circuit, as well as the club circuit, and engage in shows of any level. The group was called Super Slave. The original members of the group from left, as in the below photo were:

*Winston Blackett, Keyboards; Michael Cheeseman, Guitar/ Lead Vocals; Andrea Barker, Lead Vocals; Andy Weekes, Drums/Lead Vocals; Obrian Thomas, Saxohones/Lead Vocals; Charlie King, Bass/Lead Vocals and Ricky Brathwaite, Trumpet/Flugelhorn/Lead Vocals [Band Leader].*

# Chapter 6

## On the Road Again: Germany

Fate would have it that one night in 1980, after the band's nightly performance at Paradise Hotel, Barbados, a German agent by the name of Derek Wilkie came over to the band and asked to meet with the two horn players. We sat for about thirty minutes with the agent who expressed his interest in having the horn players [Ricky Brathwaite and O'brien Thomas] join an already established Bajan band living in Germany called Caribbean Rhapsody. I turned it down immediately, but O'Brian Thomas, "Thomo", as he was affectionately called, decided he was not turning down such an opportunity. There were no other saxophone players on the Island, at the time, to match Thomo's musical standard. This left me in a very precarious position. After some discussion with "Thomo" and with the entire band, Thomo and I decided we would transfer all of our shares and equipment to the other band members, with no cost attached, so that the band could continue without us. While they thought it was a nice gesture, they just did not have the spirit and will to continue, so the group decided to disband.

Thomo and I eventually joined the band, along with Brian Walker, another former member of the band, Outfit. The name of the band was changed from Caribbean Rhapsody to Rhapsody.

The members from left:
*Wayne Gittens, bass; Obrian Thomas, saxophones/lead vocals/percussion; Brian Walker, keyboards/lead vocals;; Leo Murphy, drums; Michael Cheeseman, lead guitar/lead vocals/percussion; Andrew Murphy, rhythm guitar/lead vocals and Ricky Brathwaite, trumpet/flugelhorn/percussion and lead vocals.*

The band was well received in Germany, performing approximately 200 shows per year. The band also did studio recordings and TV shows. The photo below shows me as lead vocalist on a major TV show in Hamburg, Germany. The song was one that was written for Rhapsody, as well as the popular group Air Supply.

So dynamic and versatile was the group that we performed at prestigious jazz clubs in Berlin Germany, such as Quazi Moto.

German TV Studio

Vinyl Jacket Cover-1982

At lot of the band's success was not based only on musical performance, but the way the band dressed as well.

In 1982, the band Rhapsody was invited to a German studio called "Sinus Studios" to engage in a song recording. The writer, as I understood it was British. Our agency facilitated this recording process about a year after the song was assigned to us. It took a full year to pursue this venture, because we could not accumulate the funds nor time to go into the studio. Once we were able to do so, the common consensus was to record an original song written by the band members entitled "Anything after You", along with "Every Woman in The World". The former was recorded first. The latter, I did the lead vocals. It was rather strange how that came about, even though I did do lead vocals at live performances. The main vocalist in the band, Andrew Murphy, was preparing to enter the performance room to record the lead vocals. However, after the horns had completed the first song and I was packing up my trumpet, I was asked to check the vocal microphone.

I began by the customary: testing 1-2-3 and repeated a few times. The producer asked if I could sing into the microphone. I knew the chorus to Every Woman, so I began to sing it. I realized from looking through the glass separating the control room from the performance room, that there was some unusual discussion taking place. The producer, through the talkback microphone, asked if I knew the words to the song. I responded that I only knew the chorus. I was summoned to the control room. When I got into the room, I was given the lyrics on a sheet of paper and told to give the recording a shot. I did not object, though there was a strange look on the lead vocalist's face.

I returned to the performance room and proceeded to sing the song. I could tell that the people in the control room liked what they were hearing. There were more discussions from inside the control room. I was then officially told that I was selected to sing the song and that my voice was the one they were in search of. The rest is history.

About eight months after the recording I was on my way downstairs to the kitchen from my bedroom. I heard the song on the radio and became very emotional. I shouted and alerted the other band members present that our song was on the radio. A more critical examination revealed that the voice on that particular version was indeed not mine. Further interrogation revealed that this was not the band's recording period.

We made several telephone calls and were finally told that the writer of the song had given several other bands the authorization to use the song. The version we heard on the radio was by the British-

Australian Group, Air Supply -- a new band that was gaining momentum on the charts. Both the German and British media admitted that they preferred our version, which featured a pop genre with a reggae slant in the chorus, but had to go with Air Supply's version. This is because the group "Air Supply" was more known and people tended to gravitate towards the first version they hear. This was really heart breaking for us, but there was little we could do. We had to pick ourselves up, dust ourselves off, and keep going.

Germany was interesting in the sense that my initial ideology about Germany was masked by the frequent locally televised shows of war between The USA and Germany. Once I set foot on German soil, I realized that it was extremely technologically advanced over other metropolitan countries. Berlin especially, was analogous to a fairytale book: the exotic cars, stores, restaurants, and hotels etc. The people were quite nice but were very rigid when it came to being on time. Everything started on time. Trains and buses left at exactly the scheduled time. I can remember that I was supposed to meet a girlfriend at 4 p.m., at a particular venue, and reached at 4:15 p.m. She had left. When asked, after the fact, if she could not wait 15 minutes. She chuckled and said, "I said 4 p.m., not 4:15 p.m."

West Germany was a cultural shock. The band would drive, on occasion from West Germany to Berlin. While I loved West Germany, I adored Berlin. The band Rhapsody was assigned a big bus, which housed nine persons comfortably, along with all of our sound and musical equipment. At that time, only four of us held German drivers' licenses. I was one of those persons along with band manager

Rudy Murphy, guitarist/vocalist Andrew Murphy and sound engineer Dereck Joseph. The below photo shows me in preparation to board the driver's seat of the bus on a trip to Berlin. The trip to berlin was approximately 9 hours long, and very tedious. Most of the time, after three hours, only a few members would be awake thus creating a sense of loneliness for whoever is trusted with the task of the long journey.

## Berlin Wall

We would always dread or arrival to the boarder which was partitioned by the then Berlin Wall. It is my understanding that this wall was structured by East Germany to prevent East Germans from fleeing to West Germany. Once we crossed the border, there was some degree of tension until we reach our destination. Helicopters escorted us for the entire journey. Departing from East Germany to the West Germany was even more contentious, because the soldiers would unpack our equipment – sometimes even dismantling the back of our speaker boxes in search of possible escapees. It was that serious.

## Gun Point

In fact, on one of our first trips to Berlin, as soon as we reached the boarder, soldiers checked the entire bus, even under the bottom with metal detectors. The process was so long that after driving for so many hours, I felt the urgent need to go to the bathroom. I saw one of the soldiers quietly standing near the bus with what I thought was a cool demeanor. The band members suggested that I approach the soldier with caution and no sudden moves. I approached the front door attempting to explain the need to go to a bathroom. I saw aggression like never before. The soldier aggressively shouted very loudly in German to stay on the bus, while simultaneously pointing his rifle directly in my face. I was told, after the fact that people are shot at that same location quite frequently. For some reason I felt no sense of fear at that point, but it certainly set in as we continued on our way. I understood a small bit of German, but did not understand a word he was saying. I slowly retraced my steps while retaining eye contact with the soldier. The soldier also kept his eyes on my every move until we were allowed to depart. Pulling up by the side of the road to urinate was not a good idea. I had to hold that thought for another 45 minutes or so. We had no further encounters of that kind us to our destination in Berlin. The people and the gig turned out to be very pleasant. We eventually got back to West Germany in good spirits, occupying our thoughts with the narratives of how drastically different the East was from the West. What affected us even more than the boarder ordeal was how infectious Caribbean music was and its impact on the German audience. We were able to intimidate some of the finest German jazz musicians, in an internationally known jazz space through our music. Intimidation? Yes. The jazz musicians did tell us that it was difficult to compete with what we were playing, not fully grasping what it was.

## Hamburg

Not long after we returned from Berlin we were off to another gig. This one turned out to be another strange experience. The band, Rhapsody drove miles to a gig in a beautiful city called Hamburg. This was our first gig in Hamburg. The city was very beautiful. Similar to Berlin, there were all types of shops, from electronic to strip clubs. We were warned by the agency to be careful in this city.

One day the keyboardist, Brian Walker and I, thought we would explore the town because we were leaving the following day. While walking along a busy shopping area we saw this man in the street fretting that there were girls there, girls everywhere and nobody was patronizing his club. He was literally begging us to come in for free. I remembered that we were warned not to let our guards down in this city. I reminded Brian of this. He however insisted that he was taking a peep, with or without me. On entering the club, I realized there was a naked white girl dancing on stage. We had never witnessed such before, so Brian convinced me to explore for a few minutes. On entering, we were escorted to a horseshoe type seating with a table in the center. The dancer immediately left the stage, slipped on a black coat over her nude body and joined us at the table. She asked if we could treat her to a glass of wine. I could see the excitement on Brian's face, and he signaled to the bartender that he wanted a bottle of wine. I tried to get Brian's attention without fanfare, but he became very engaged with the dancer. Brian was aware that I did not drink alcohol but ignored me completely. I ordered a coke. Before we could get comfortable, two very big guys joined us at both ends of the horseshoe couch and blocked us in from both ends. The bartender brought the drinks tab over and placed it on the table in front of me. I slowly picked it up and looked at the amount. The amount was DM$800.00. I pointed out to the bartender that the point was inaccurately positioned. He responded it was correct. I knew that there was trouble brewing. I only had about DM$300.00 in my pocket. Brian urged me not to worry that he had about DM$1,000.00 on him. Before we could pay, the two men, we believed were 'bouncers', grabbed both Brian and me by the scruff of our necks, emptied our pockets of about DM$1,400.00 in total, guided us to the door and pushed us out of the club on to the street.

We did not fight back but looked to see if a police officer was nearby. We saw a police officer walking the beat. We approached him and explained what had transpired. He accompanied us back to the club. To our amazement, there was only one person in the club — a different bartender. He swore to the police that we were mistaken, because he had never seen us before, and he was the only employee on duty until his shift changed in an hour. We felt compromised, humiliated, and violated. The police stated that he could do nothing to help us at this point, but we were free to bring charges against the owner, if we could prove our case. This was certainly not practical. The officer left warning us to be careful in Hamburg because tourists were often preyed on as targets.

I was so angry that I did not utter a word until we got back to the hotel. At that point, I explained the entire scenario to the other band members, who rubbed in the fact that we were forewarned and deserved every bit of what we encountered. That was just a bad experience, but living and touring Germany was quite exciting and overall it was a great experience. There were poor moments of reflection as well.

## Car Crash

The band lived for some time in a small town called Sinsheim. I bought a Volkswagen Beetle for less than two thousand Deutsche Marks (U.S $1,000). The vehicle was like new, because vehicles are not only valued in Germany by their condition, but mileage. This particular day in 1983, I got a call from two German female friends who were leaving Germany on holiday for Barbados the following day. They had asked if I had anything that I wanted them to take to Barbados for a family member or friend. I did give it some thought but did not want to burden them.

The day of their travel, they called to say goodbye and that they would be on vacation for two weeks. They said that their flight was leaving in three hours and I could still get anything to them once I did it within an hour. I discussed it with the keyboardist in the band, Brian Walker, who thought I was cutting it a little too close, in terms of time. My friends lived in a nearby town that took about thirty minutes via the autobahn (highway), or 45 to 1 hour by what we referred to as the back road. I remember Brian suggesting quite aggressively that I forget about the trip because it seemed too last minute. I had already told the girls that I was on my way to deliver the package for my mother. Again, Brian expressed his concern about the rush around, and went further, suggesting that I will call back to say that I had crashed. I ignored Brian and decided that I would not waste any more time and left right away taking the backroad.

I remember driving slightly faster than normal. About 15 minutes before reaching the nearby town where the girls resided, as I went around a sharp bend in the road, I was shocked, encountering a slippery wet road. In other words, the sun was shining brightly until I reached the bend. I panicked and hit the brakes too suddenly. I slid from one side to the next and barely missed an old lady crossing the road, by a coat of paint. I ended up knocking down a guard wall and came to a stop in somebody's yard.

I slowly emerged from the vehicle honestly thinking that I was dead. When I looked at the car, it was difficult to understand how anyone could emerge from it without being seriously injured. The car was a wreck and I emerged without a scratch. In a short space of time scores of people had gathered, and angry ones. They were becoming very aggressive and pointed their fingers at me. I did not know enough German to understand what they were saying, but I could tell that it was only a matter of time before they beat me up. I just stood there in awe until a gentleman opened his door and motioned to me to hurry up and come in. I capitalized on the good gesture. The man and his wife spoke very little English, but enough that I could communicate. He allowed me to make phone calls to my girlfriends who were not far away, and to the band house.

When I called home, Brian answer the phone and without hesitation in Bajan dialect asked "Wait…you crash fuh trute boy?" I responded in the affirmative and explained where the accident occurred. In a short space of time, my girlfriends and Brian appeared on the scene. Shortly after the police arrived as well.

The police transported me to the police station to fill out an accident report. I was charged DM$3,000 for the damage caused and that was it. I then had to spend another DM$1,500 on my crashed car to restore it to an even better state than it was in initially. I would never forget that scary episode. To this day, I still feel a slight sense of nervousness everything I drive around a bend that is wet from rainfall. There are other moments of reflection from experiences, some pleasant, some not so pleasant, coming out of my three-year touring stint living in West Germany.

## Boney M's Manager

The Bajan Band, Rhapsody, was rapidly becoming a household name in Germany. The band performed at the finest and most prestigious venues across West and East Germany. During that period, horn players were struggling, because new releases did not have horns, so horn players had to find other ways of survival. As a result, I studied percussion, played congas and timbales, and became one of the lead vocalists in the band. I always saw myself as a team player and band person, rather than a solo artist.

One afternoon, the then manager, of a mega group called Boney M contacted me. He announced himself as Frank Farian and said he was calling from Frankfurt, Germany. At the time, as earlier mentioned, the band Rhapsody resided in a small town called Heidelberg. He said he wanted to have a serious conversation with me and asked if we could do it on the phone. I had known of the group Boney M and the crowds they generated. He explained that he had seen the band on a few occasions and that he could make me a millionaire if I would agree to go solo. He went on to suggest that the band was stifling my progress and success. The truth is, first, I really liked the composition and camaraderie of the band; second, I was scared to take the risk, because I did not believe I possessed the qualities Frank saw in me. Frank suggested that I take some time to give it serious thought. He asked me to record his phone number and call him when I had decided. I was hesitant to discuss it with any member of the band for fear of being labeled a traitor or unconsciously planting any seed of mistrust that could destroy a good thing. I never returned the call and I never heard back from manager, Frank Farian. I always wondered, though, what might have been the outcome had I accepted the challenge. I am aware though that the group Boney M, some years later found themselves in trouble for miming and lip-syncing and not actually singing at their live concerts.

## Clash of Ideals

Before I migrated to Germany, I had met Juel Yearwood, a girlfriend who appeared to show much interest in my musical career. Her father, who was from the Parish of St. John, is said to be partly responsible for the success of Prime Minister Errol Barrow, Barbados' first prime Minister and father of our Independence.

Juel was raised in a totally different environment than I was, and therefore this would have put considerable strain on our relationship. Her mother thought I was a nice person, while her father, John, did not believe that I was suitable for his daughter, and this was no doubt, demonstrated.

Once I migrated to Germany, Juel expressed her desire to be with me and was willing to give up her luxurious life in Barbados to do so. I tried to convince her that if she did come to Germany she would live a stifled life, because she would not be allowed to work. She did not seem to care once I was working for enough money to support her.

One day as the band was preparing to 'hit' the road for Berlin, I got a call from Juel. Her words were, "I am coming up there now." I did not understand what she meant, until she explained that she was at the airport in Barbados getting ready to board a Lufthansa airline in route to Germany. She gave me the flight details indicating that she was serious. I explained that I would not be in West Germany when she arrived but would commission a female German friend to pick her up at Frankfurt Airport, what she should do to be recognized, and that she would have to stay with my friend Andrea for the entire week that I would be away.

On my return from Berlin, I realized that Juel had travelled with most of her wardrobe and several boxes of toiletries, cosmetics etc. Juel made it clear that she had resigned from her job in Barbados and had no immediate plans on returning. Initially, I was not comfortable with her decision because there was no discussion on this sensitive area. Anyway, after a bit of tension, explanation and pleading, I embraced the idea and we were happy together – at least for a while. I took Juel with me to many gigs, once there was room in our touring bus.

After about nine months living in Germany, Juel looked me full in my eyes and asked in a serious tone of voice …"Do you plan to do this for the rest of your life?" I was not sure if I understood the question. She made it even clearer in asking if I was going to play music for the rest of life. This came as quite a shock and triggered a few red flags. What started out as an amicable discussion progressively turned into a verbal fight. Our relationship seemed to have gradually deteriorated thereafter. The band's direction at that time was also out of alignment with mine and that relationship weakened as well. I ended up resigning from the band and moving to nearby Austria for a few months, while Juel remained in Germany, in search of greener pastures. Gigs were not as forthcoming as in Germany, and the entire vibe, including a strange form of the German language felt a bit out of sorts. I returned to Germany where I was approached by my German friend, Adel, who was planning her debut modeling show.

## A Runway Model?

The band Rhapsody spent very little time in our hometown of Heidelberg. The band toured all year around. In fact, we performed almost five times a week in some of the most remote towns. Our friends in Heidelberg were always elated when we were back in town. My white female German friend, Adel, was one of those persons who would spend much time hanging out with the guys at the band's three-story house. She approached me one day and explained that she was putting on her first modeling show and wanted to know if I would be interested in helping her out as one of the male models. She sought to convince me to try something different, outside of music, and said the German audience would love me.

I thought…is she crazy? The above photo shows both Adel and I modeling for the first time. I have my fair share of nerves doing what I love on stage. I have not yet managed that aspect, and now I am supposed to engage in the runaway. Anyway, I decided to give it a shot, as also shown in the below photos.

I turned out much better than I thought. My afro hairstyle was apparently the highlight of the night. I was convinced to try the modeling thing then, but I was pretty darn certain that it would have been my first and also my last episode as any kind of model.

# *Chapter 7*

---

## BACK IN BIM

### You Have to Study – Maybe Jazz?

Juel and I returned to Barbados. We thought that this was the most logical option at the time. On returning to Barbados, Juel's immediate family placed serious strain on the relationship believing that I brought no feasible economic plan to the development of their daughter's life, being a musician. The relationship finally cracked under the pressure and eventually broke up. Unfortunately, we did not keep in touch, but remained good friends, even though I had not seen or heard from her for quite a few years. I remember, quite vividly, though, her last words to me before we parted each other's company in tears ..."You are so intelligent, and I know you believe in your music, but it would not take anything away from you if you added academic studies to your musical career." I dismissed that notion immediately and quietly walked away, because I believed that she was following in the same direction as her family, which was responsible for the relationship's demise, in the first place – not thinking that playing music was a real job. Those final words have played a significant role in my life up to this present day.

Strangely enough, Bassist, Linus Yaw contacted me and strongly suggested that I start playing jazz, that he had a concept for a jazz concert at the prestigious Frank Collymore Hall in Barbados. He did organize the concert with some of the finest exponents of the art form. In fact, I was the least experienced, jazz-wise in the band.

The band consisted of percussionist, "El Vernon Del Congo" (Vern Best); bassist, Linus Yaw; pianist, Adrian Clarke; drummer, Antonio "Boo" Rudder; saxophonist, Andre Woodvine and me on trumpet. The master of ceremonies, Carl Moore, announced the individual members of the band with all sorts of profound adjectives. When he introduced me, it was like 'B double-flat'. In a subdued tone of voice, he mumbled…"on trumpet, Ricky Brathwaite," Every member, once introduced, played a short solo in recognition. I refused to be so disrespected. After all, I might not have been known as a jazz player but was a houschold name as an arranger and producer. In fact, the year prior (1985) I had arranged one of the biggest songs to come out of Barbados — "Sousie". The night, however, was a good night regardless. I was well received as a newcomer to the jazz art form by the well-attended audience.

After the show, and as I was packing away my trumpet and flugelhorn, I realized that there was an attractive lady who remained sitting in the hall. She seemed to be trying to get my attention. Because of the lighting in the hall, I could not make out her features. I drew closer and realized the face was that of Juel's. She motioned to me by her waving hand to come over. I walked slowly over to where she was sitting. When I got within about three feet, she softly asked me, with a nonchalant look on her face, to sit next to her. She explained why she stayed back. I was not sure what the conversation would be about, but was hoping that it would not be about rekindling a relationship that had ended many years ago.

She spoke to me like a head teacher and made it clear that she did not like the way I was introduced by the MC. She quipped that she was happy that I did not play when I was introduced. She claimed that the rest of the audience was affected in the same way that she was, and that it was not her imagination. After a short discussion, she said she thought I was the highlight of the night and suggested that I should never be so disrespected again. She passionately admonished that I should seriously consider going overseas and pursuing studies in music. She opined, "This is the only way that you would be able to command respect in this little myopic country (Barbados). This resonated with me for weeks after. In fact, Juel's words returned to haunt me many years after. Those words might have been the seed that allowed me to reap scholarships in the USA from 1988 onwards. Unfortunately, Juel died in 1990 at the age of 42 from unusual breathing complications.

I still thank her today for believing in me and seeing other talents and gifts in me that I did not even see in myself.

# Chapter 8

## The Barbados Hotel Circuit

The hotel circuit in Barbados has never been a progressive one from a musical perspective, but it has been a life source for many entertainers. The Food and Beverage managers have traditionally been assigned the responsibility for nightly entertainment. Some of them could not differentiate between the Sea and Top-C. Sometimes it was more the case of performing for those managers than the hotels' guests.

"Lord Radio" (Oliver Brome) would have performed for years at the major hotels in Barbados and made an exceptional living. At one point, he was forced to form three bands: Bimshire Boys, Melody Masters and Sophisticated Sounds. This was in an effort to fill the void for quality shows and appropriate music. "Lord Radio", although focused on the hotel circuit, became a household name, a successful businessman and a Bajan Icon.

On my return to Barbados in 1978, after a successful tour of Canada, "Lord Radio" heard that I was back in the country. He called me up and with an assertive tone of voice and few words commanded, "Ricky, it is Lord Radio. Go up to Sam Lord's Castle hotel tonight." He hung up the phone before I could get the necessary information. I called his son Arthur Brome, who confirmed that Lord Radio's band Sophisticated Sounds was playing at Sam Lord's Castle. Arthur was also the guitarist in the band. I indicated to him that I did not have access to private transportation, since the hotel was located extreme south to where I was living. I enquired as to if I could get a ride with him, since he lived very close to where I lived. I was told that I would have to get in the path of his route, and this is where I would also be dropped off after the gig. I had to walk for a about a mile before and after the gig. The band played 7 nights per week at a fee of Bds $75 per night. This was not a bad pay packet for that period. I thought…There was nowhere else to go from there, I thought, because horn players and drummers were becoming 'extinct'. Other musicians on the club circuit laughed at the fact that I was playing with what they perceived as a digressive hotel band. After all, I had recently engaged in an impressive showing, weeks prior, with the Canadian based Bajan band, The Outfit.

There were times when I honestly felt embarrassed, but the pay was my ultimate motivation. Some of the musicians who laughed at me had financial issues and could not visit the supermarket as often as I did. Conversely, musicians performing nightly on the hotel circuit also laughed at the musicians who performed on the Club and

Nightclub circuit. They took more risks and sometimes were not sure of when and from where the next pay cheque would emerge.

Strange enough, I learned a great deal from playing with Lord Radio and his band, Sophisticated Sounds. Most bands practiced a song in a given key, and that never changed. However, I soon realized this was not the case with Sophisticated Sounds. Any night that Lord Radio was not in fine voice, he would move around the key accordingly. As a matter of fact, Lord Radio on occasion would actually call the key and begin to sing, without hearing a reference chord or key tone. Band members were always amazed at how someone who does not play an instrument could execute such. It was pure genius.

## Holiday Inn Hotel

One night, during a show, Lord Radio came on stage, cleared his voice, glanced back at the band and shouted: "Yellow Bird in E." and started to sing. Of course, the band without question began following Lord Radio's lead. The melody of the song "Yellow Bird" was already challenging, furthermore in the key of F sharp ($F^{\#}$) Major for the trumpet. After a verse and chorus, Lord Radio pointed his finger to me suggesting that I improvise or play the melody for the verse and chorus before he re-entered. It was embarrassing. I struggled through the entire form. Both improvising and playing the melody were disastrous. I could see the rest of the band chuckling from the corners of my eyes. When the band took a break after the show, Lord

Radio walked over to me in front of the other band members and aggressively equipped, “You thought you could play, huh?... “You only learn to play when you pass through my band!” The other band members laughed even more openly. This was a learning curve for me: learn to play any song in different keys.

## Missed Opportunity

Performing with Lord Radio allowed me to see or meet a few international superstars. Jazz vocalist, Sarah Vaughn was one of them. This particular night the band Sophisticated Sound was playing at the prestigious Sandy Lane Hotel along with the internationally acclaimed, Sandy Lane Strings. The Sandy Lane Strings was the house band for the Sandy Lane Hotel for about 30 years, at that point. They had become very popular outside of Barbados, because icons visiting the hotel would go back to their countries and communicate fond memories of Barbados as well as the band. The leader of the band was a talented jazz guitarist icon, Clifton Glasgow, who often mesmerized great musicians from around the world.

That night after the band’s first set, the rhythm guitarist, Winston Greene, walked over to me and indicated that there was an older lady sitting at a particular table in the hotel restaurant who wanted to meet me. I enquired as to who this older lady was. I was told ‘the great Sarah Vaughn’. I was a teenager at the time, had no idea about jazz, and had never heard about Sarah Vaughn, so I immediately declined.

At the end of the night, there was a short discussion where I was scolded by other band members for not showing respect to the 'superstar'. My initial thought, based on how the information was delivered to me, was that it was an older woman who wanted to hit on a young boy. Anyway, part of the post discussion was that she believed that I had the potential to be a great trumpet player. Apparently, she told the small section of the band attending her table that I sounded like a mixture of two great American jazz trumpeters: Clifford Brown and Freddie Hubbard. The latter I met while studying in the USA. The irony of the situation was that I had never heard of them either. Playing with Lord Radio's bands equipped me not only with the ability to navigate around different keys and meet vacationing superstars, but learning to play the keyboards and sharpening my vocal skills as well.

## Digital Transition

As earlier mentioned, with the advent of modern digital technology, horn players found difficulty in securing gigs. Keyboard synthetic horn tones had taken over. In order to survive, musically, and secure a spot in the band, I began singing lead in some songs, while playing the trumpet only as a special feature. That is where I also learned to play the keyboards, at least only with one hand, when the band's keyboard player quit at short notice. In a few months, I eventually became the lead vocalist in the band, replacing two icons, Midge Springer and Hubert Grant, who had spent quite a few years performing with the band. This gave me the false security of my significance in the band.

## Fired

The band members would continuously complain to the boss (Lord Radio), about me not assisting in lifting equipment after gigs. I tried to explain that I would prefer to take a nightly pay cut rather than hurt my fingers or hand lifting equipment. Lord Radio made it absolutely clear that there was only one star in his band, and I was expected to lift equipment like the other members of the band. I stood my ground and Lord Radio stood his. One day I heard a loud car horn outside of my house. I looked out and realized that it was the boss. I went outside to him; he gave me a book to sign for my weekly wage and fired me on the spot. No reason or dialogue of the termination was had. Lord Radio kept his eyes forward the entire time, and as soon as I was finished signing the book, he handed me my wages, in cash, and immediately drove off without uttering another word.

I was devastated. The music scene in Barbados was a nightmare and it was difficult to secure gigs on the Barbados hotel circuit. I could not imagine how I would survive as a musician.

## Compassionate Lord Radio

About two weeks after I my departure from the band, Sophisticated Sound, I heard a loud horn blowing outside my house. I looked through my bedroom window and recognized it was Lord Radio's van. He managed to spot me as I was pulling back the curtain. He shouted in raw Bajan dialect "Yuh gine stop there peeping at me or yuh gine cum outside?" I was only wearing shorts at the time. I made my way outside, and before I could say good morning, he asked me to get into the front seat of his van. I tried to apologize for not being appropriately dressed, but he too apologized for dropping in unannounced.

I was not sure what the visit was about, but he immediately suggested that I put together my own band. As he put it, "You don't need to be in anybody's band. You are quite talented. Start controlling your own destiny. This was some of the best advice I had ever been given. He also promised me that as soon as I can get the musicians together he would set up whatever equipment I request, including transportation of equipment to and from all gigs for a modest fee of Barbados $150 per night – US $75 per night. This was an unbelievable gesture. So said, so done.

# Kaiyo The Band

## Kaiyo a new group but quite impressive

The local music scene has been going through a very trying time for over five years and many factors are responsible ranging from low hotel fees for bands; the high cost of musical equipment to the end of the dance era.

Unlike the mid-70s when Barbados could boast of bands such as the **Troubadours**, **BRC Outfit**, **Organisation**, **Lunar 7**, **Harmony**, **Brothers** and the **Music Circle** among many others, one is now able to count all the local bands on both hands.

It is therefore surprising when a new band emerges on the local scene with outstanding and experienced musicians. One such band is **Kaiyo**.

**Kaiyo** was formed 10 months ago by Barbados' top rumpeter and outstanding musician Ricky (Little Ricky) Brathwaite. Managed initially by Maxie Baldeo of MaxiMusic, **Kaiyo** comprised along with Ricky on trumpet, keyboards and vocals, Michael Richards on trombone, percussion and background vocals, Ranny Lavine on drums, Charlie King on bass and vocals and Michael Hope on guitar and vocals.

In three months of performing on the hotel circuit the band not only became "the talk of the town," but recorded its first song in December last year called Xmas Time.

This song showed the outstanding abilities of leader and arranger of **Kaiyo**, Ricky who also wrote and sang the song. **Xmas Time** also showed the talent of the musicians, especially the "biting horn section."

Despite the initial success of **Kaiyo**, the band went through some early changes. Bass player Charlie King left the group and as well as trombonist Michael Richards who has not been playing much this year.

**Kaiyo**, however has grown from strength to strength. Having an outstanding season with Battleground Calypso Tent, **Kaiyo** with the added horn section was the best Tent Band for 1985.

The calypso season was also a success for band leader Little Ricky who was musical director for the tent and also the arranger of the Tune of the Crop, **ore Grynner More** and the outstanding **Sousie** by the Director.

With the Crop Over season completed, **Kaiyo** is now forced to concentrate on the hotel circuit and indeed adapt to the change of music and style. This has resulted in some transformation in the structure of the group.

Leslie Patterson, Richard Stoute Teen Talent star now on bass and vocals, another Richard Stoute teenage star, Brian Carter is on vocals and drummer Ranny Lavine has been replaced for the hotels by an electronic drum machine.

**From left to right are Michael Hope — guit and vocals; Ricky Brathwaite — trump**

I called up a few musicians with whom I got along well. Those musicians, as reflected in the provided press release are from bottom: Michael Hope, guitar; Ricky Brathwaite, trumpet, keyboards and band leader/manager; Brian Carter, lead vocals; and Leslie Patterson, bass and lead vocals. Missing is the electric Japanese drummer - Korg DD50 drum machine. Below is an updated later version of the band Kaiyo.

*From left: Guitarist, Michael "Hopie" Hope; Drums, the late, Randolph "Ranny" Lavine; Bass/vocals, Charlie King; Trumpet/fugel horn/vocals, Ricky Brathwaite and Trombone, Michael Richards.*

The hotels did not pay very well, therefore the group was kept as practically small as possible, without compromising too much of the musical quality. I cannot recall how the name of the band, Kaiyo emerged, but it quickly gained local attention. In a matter of weeks, we had secured 5 nights per week on the hotel circuit. My small Suzuki 600 car was the official transportation for the band members and their instruments.

Focusing on music was what I wanted to do, so I approached leading Barbadian sound engineer, Maxi Baldeo on managing the band. He accepted immediately and invited us to rehearse in his recording studio, just outside Bridgetown. We ended up recording one of my original songs called "Xmas Time." Shortly after, Bajan icon, Mighty Gabby invited me to perform in his popular calypso 'tent', "Battleground Calypso Tent".

# Chapter 9

## Gabby's Battleground Calypso Tent

After a year performing in the tent with an established Bajan band called Creative Sounds, Mighty Gabby became disgusted with the band. Apparently, the then bandleader and musical director, Mike Sealy, complained that the band had outlived its musical usefulness. According to Mike, they were struggling to properly and effectively play his challenging arrangements. Gabby agreed and fired the backing band, approximately one week before the official opening night of the Tent. The natural progression was to utilize my band, which was available on the weekends, and augment the rhythm section with older, seasoned sight-reading horn players from the Police Band.

Gabby asked me if I would accept the role of bandleader for the tent. I gladly accepted. The rhythm section was strong, but was slow on reading musical notation, so I worked a little overtime.

Even though I did not have the official title of manager, I was pretty much involved in most goings on in the tent. There were times when I got to the venue early and discovered that there were no chairs laid for the patrons. On reporting this, I would end up as the person to make the arrangements or follow up arrangements to have the chairs brought to the venue. I was extremely committed to both Gabby and his 'Tent". I was therefore mandated by "Gabby" with the full responsibility of sourcing the band members, rehearsing the calypsonians and anything else that contributes to the success of the 'Tent". I was therefore very instrumental in assisting in the guidance of everyone represented in the Tent. Some calypsonians appreciated my input while others did not. I remember one incident in 1996 during one of our nightly performances that was met with different responses.

## Michael "Director" Forde

"Director" had, one year earlier, written and sung one of the greatest songs to come out of Barbados in 1985. In fact, the song "Sousie" which was arranged by me and produced by international icon, Eddy Grant, is labeled as the unofficial anthem of Barbados.

I would have spoken to Director on a few occasions about one of the songs he wrote and seemed to struggle in performing it. The name of the song was "Aware Africa". It appeared to the band, fellow calypsonians, the patrons, and myself, as though Director was developing the song on a nightly basis, as he performed it. The resentment for the song showed on the patrons faces as he performed it nightly. The other thing is that he was not consistent in the number of verses the song consisted of. This meant that I, as the musical director, had to be guessing on where to cut the band from night to night. I would have to watch Director closely to determine where the song ended.

I tried to have a cordial discussion with Director to determine how many verses the song had, and if we could reexamine the melody of the song etc. Michael "Director" Forde's response to me was …"I can't commit to any number of verses the song has right now. If I feel like singing three, four or five verses that is my prerogative." He then aggressively walked away.

On one particular show night, Director came on stage and sung four verses. One could see the boredom on the patrons faces. In fact, he was crippling the mood of the night. After Director sang, what I believed to be the fourth and final verse, I cut the band. I then realized that he was about to sing a fifth verse. It was quite embarrassing for him as the singer, me as musical director, and some members of the backing band. Director turned around from the front of the stage and looked at me with an angry face as though he would fight. It also seemed as though he did not intend to move unless he was allowed to sing another verse. I stood my ground and did not direct the band to continue.

Director gave a short speech to the audience explaining that he came to perform for them so that they could have a good time, but the MD prevented him from doing so. I was fearful, at this point, that the audience would jeer or boo me. Instead, most of the patrons were quiet while others motioned to Director to leave the stage. This incident has been etched in the front of my mind from 1986 until now.

## An Arranger in the Making

About two years after, one of the leading calypsonians in Gabby's Battleground Tent, "Mighty Grynner" (McDonald Blenman), had some challenges getting his music from his arranger for opening night, which was about 5 days away. Gabby approached me with a cassette tape of the two songs – "Stinging Bees" and "Gabby's Controversy", and insisted that I go home, as a matter of urgency and arranged the two songs. I explained to Mighty Gabby that I did not have a clue of the first steps of arranging music. Gabby insisted that I try, because the Tent would be a disaster if it started without "Mighty Grynner". It took me at least 24 hours on each song, and in those days there was no way in knowing how the song would actually sound before band rehearsal.

The songs were instant hits within the Tent environs and beyond. I have to thank Gabby (Anthony Carter), for his confidence in me, because that trust has propelled me to be the arranger and producer that I have evolved into over the years. I went on to arrange and produce for some of the bigger names in the calypso and soca arena which have produced three Crop Over monarchs: "Bumba", "They Want to Know" and "Love Your Own" 1997; Aziza, "One People, One Nation" 2016; and "Classic" with his inaugural "One song" 2019.

## The Demise of Battleground Tent

The Tent was where I grew and developed as an arranger. As earlier mentioned, I emerged as the main arranger in the Tent and beyond, arranging for other big names in Calypso such as: "Mighty Gabby", "Grynner", "Romeo", "Poonka", "Invader #3", "Mighty Dragon", "Mighty Carew", "Rouser", "Black Pawn", "Mighty Whitey", "Pompey", Colin Spencer, and Kid Site among others.

The home for the Tent was the Democratic Labour Party [DLP] Auditorium in George Street, Belleville, Barbados. The show normally started at 8 p.m. It was the most popular of Tents at the time. It catered to a wide cross section of patrons, and was a place where one could detox after a hard day at work through a mixture of serious social and political commentary calypsos and laughter. So successful was the Tent that in order to gain advantage in seating, patrons had to be seated by 7 p.m. Gabby's Battle Ground Calypso Tent was forced to turn back some 50 to 100 patrons on weekends, until the season was in full swing, then the Tent would increase to 5 days per week. There were times when the Tent would produce shows for an entire week and was still forced to turn back patrons each night, because of the hall's capacity to accommodate only 800 to 900 persons seated.

I became a member of the Tent in 1983 and enjoyed every moment of the Tent, which seemed so well organized. Mighty Gabby and I had developed a great relationship and friendship through the years, even though we did not see eye to eye on some musical issues, which on occasion led to quarrels. However, I still believe that Gabby made a colossal error that caused the demise of the Tent, which was in full flight. There was great chemistry between Gabby, myself, my band and the calypsonians.

Unfortunately or fortunately, Gabby was invited in 1984 by the iconic Mighty Sparrow (Slinger Francisco) to perform as a guest calypsonian in his Tent in Trinidad. "Mighty Sparrow" is considered by many as the world's greatest calypsonian.

Gabby accepted. On his return from Trinidad, he seemed a bit more serious and not the jovial Gabby I had come to know. The Trinidad experience had created a more business-like Gabby who decided to have his own dressing room upstairs of the auditorium, while everyone else had to settle for a dressing room downstairs. Everyone, except Gabby realized the isolation and segregation that this had created. I thought I would approach Gabby on this new and unwelcomed behavior. I can remember quite vividly the conversation that ensued. What was etched in the back of my mind was when Gabby said to me… "Rick, this is not a Tent. We are making mock sport. You would have to go to a Tent in Trinidad to see what a real Tent is supposed to be like. I am the star in this Tent and this is how I want it to be from today onwards."

In addition, Gabby informed me that he would be dismissing all of the comical calypsonians from the Tent such as "Nubian", "Rubber Man" and "Cubba". These special acts provided lighter moments to the show with laughter, rather than the constant focus on the ills of the country, and the divisive tactics of the government in power etc. He exclaimed that he wanted the Tent to be a serious Tent. I was so shocked that I stood there just staring at him. Then I developed the courage and responded, "Gabby, you have allowed your experience in Trinidad with the Mighty Sparrow to destroy the Tent." Gabby, without hesitation responded, "No Rick. Watch and see." Well… I watched and observed for two years after that there was a definite fall off in attendance.

## Calypso Tent Coup

In 1987, some of the more established calypsonians, through frustration in the new direction, noticeable drop in patronage, lack of performance fees and broken synergies, invited me to a special meeting to discuss the way forward. I asked if Gabby was a part of the special meeting, and was told no. I accepted the invitation, but informed Gabby on what was transpiring. Gabby showed up at the meeting like a man possessed, dressed in full army camouflage attire and serious as a judge. All present looked totally shocked to see Gabby present at the meeting. At this time, I explained that I invited Gabby to the meeting, because any way forward should include Gabby, and out of respect, he should be briefed on why he was not invited to a meeting representing his own Tent. At this time, Gabby was extremely quiet and seemed disengaged.

The meeting started with an explanation as to why Gabby was not invited, because of similar reasons aforementioned. It was also communicated that there were plans to start a new Tent called "Battlefield Calypso Tent". This was the first time I was hearing about this new plan forward as well. Gabby interjected by saying quite calmly that he just wanted to say a few things and he would leave. One could hear a pin drop.

Gabby first thanked me for having the decency to inform him of the meeting. He went on to thank everyone present for their commitment to him and Battleground Tent over the years. With that, he gave me his special blessing and advised me that it was alright to proceed with the new Tent, "Battle Field Calypso Tent", because he would not be continuing with his "Battleground Tent". With those short comments, he departed with a forced smile on his face. There was still a strange hush in the room for a few seconds after. The meeting continued and the new Tent was formed.

## Evolution of Battlefield Calypso Tent

Battleground Calypso Tent technically continued from where "Gabby's Battleground Tent" left off, except that the band was now dressed in camouflaged uniform and berets. Peter Roy Byer had some brilliant ideas that were well executed. The very first night the Tent opened, Gabby was seated in the front row of the hall, in front of the stage. He genuinely applauded, shouted and cheered on the once Battleground Calypsonians.

My fee as Musical Director/Trumpet player with Battleground Tent was Bds$1,000 per night. Gabby had made it clear that he had never made that during his best attendance, but acknowledged that my contribution was invaluable. The new Battlefield Tent pleaded with me that the Tent was new and could not afford to pay me such a fee, so I would be offered a place on the board, which would allow me to share in any profits. I accepted.

## Ultimate Betrayal

Driving around as I do periodically, as a form of relaxation, I drove through Mansion Road, St. Michael – where I conducted weekly Tent rehearsals. I was shocked to hear a band rehearsing. I thought…I hope that band is not using my personal equipment without my approval. As I pushed the gate and entered, I was shocked to see my band was engaged in a routine Tent rehearsal without my knowledge or approval. I was not totally surprised, but the band stopped immediately and looked surprised to see me. I quietly asked what was going on. The drummer, Ronald Cummins, then a police officer, walked me outside the rehearsal room into the road. He looked confused, and from his comments seemed to have been invited to the rehearsal under the assumption that I had sanctioned it. Apparently, the same calypsonians that created the Battleground Tent coup were again at the center of another coup. After a brief conversation with the drummer on what had transpired, I reentered the rehearsal room. I expressed shock and shame at what had transpired and indicated that the band could continue the rehearsal on my equipment without charge, until they can secure other options. On investigation and talking to other Board Members, I was told that the issue was the inability to pay me such a high fee, and some of the more established calypsonians thought that it would be better to get through the rest of the season without my services or equipment. I questioned the element of dialogue over divisiveness, but was boldly told that the rehearsal was a trial run to see if it were possible to function effectively without my presence. I was disgusted with the whole procedure and decided not to continue with the Tent. The Tent reemerged the following year, but shortly after commencement, disbanded its operations without completing the annual Crop-Over season.

Working with Gabby and the Battleground Tent afforded me the opportunity to meet and work with international Vocalist, Guitarist and music producer, Eddy Grant. We have enjoyed a healthy relationship since then until today.

*From left: Eddy, Gabby and Ricky*
*[Photo: Gabby's UWI Honorary Doctorate Graduation Ceremony, 2015]*

In fact, Eddy Grant is the Executive Producer of my very first CD entitled "Supa Saf"; and as earlier mentioned Anthony "Gabby" Carter is responsible for guiding my career in the direction of becoming a musical arranger. My skills, as an arranger, came in handy in many unforeseen ways.

## Calypso Crowns: 1987, 2016 and 2019

Becoming an arranger and producer has been rewarding in the sense that, not only was I directly involved in creating many hit songs, but I have been successful in propelling three calypsonians to winning the coveted National Calypso Crown on three occasions.

In 1987, "Bumba" (Brian Payne) approached me about arranging and producing his composition for the 1987 Crop Over Festival. At that time, "Bumba" was engaged in studies at The University of The West Indies. He brought two songs in raw state: "Love Your Own" and "They Want To Know". From the time I heard the raw composition I told Bumba the song was well written, and I could hear the arrangements already. I decided to incorporate a Blues inflection and the tussle between G Major Key and its relative minor, E Minor. "Bumba" was very passionate about his lyrics and melody. The finishing touches were left to me to develop and enhance what was already great.

I convinced "Bumba" to record the song. He agreed and I hired musicians I believed would bring my ideas to fruition: Nicholas Brancker on keys and Bass; Ian "Eyan" Alleyne on Guitar; Jeffrey Grannum on Alto and tenor Saxes; and I layered a few trumpet tracks. The recording engineer was Norman Barrow, and the recording was done at the Merrymen Studios (RCA) at Searles Plantation. I wanted a hybrid sound in backing vocals between kids and adults, so I had to search for the ideal voice. That voice ended up to be that of Catherine Olivia Sandiford, a Barbadian violinist studying in the USA who was visiting from New York.

In 1916, a calypsonian by the name of "Viper" (Ewat Green) visited my recording studio with a 19-year-old seemingly shy female calypsonian by the name of Aziza (Aziza Clarke). "Viper" introduced Aziza to me and quipped that I was looking at the next Calypso Monarch. I chuckled and "Viper" made it clear that he had written this song especially for Aziza, and no one but me could arrange and produce it. He pulled out his box guitar and started strumming and singing the song. I liked it right away. I asked if Aziza knew the song, and if so, she should sing it so that I could see what I have to work with. I was impressed. I knew the key was an issue, but I liked the lyrics and melody.

Both "Viper" and myself, worked on what we were trying to achieve without any tension. Once I was clear of what "Viper" wanted to achieve, I asked Aziza to record a rough vocal track in her most suitable key so that I can start to arrange the music.

Both "Viper" and Aziza exited the studio. I found that I could not sleep at nights – constantly hearing possible arrangements. At that point, I actually started to believe that once the arrangements and lead vocal were right, it would be difficult to beat her in the competition. In a just few days, I had finished the arrangements and a fairly decent audio production. However, I did not want them to return to the studio until everything regarding the production was completed, except for the final vocal.

Aziza and "Viper" came back to the studio to hear what I had done thus far. I hid the horns and backing vocals – all done by me. Aziza was now ready for the final vocal with the belief that the other ingredients would be done at a later date. She recorded a decent vocal track from the start. She just had to be guided with certain phrases. Once we all listened back and were happy with the results, I asked to take a break while I adjusted the horns, guitar and backing vocals via my headphones. This was so that when the song "One People, One Nation" was played there would be some element of surprise.

After the short break, I asked Aziza and "Viper" if they were ready to listen critically to the production. Everyone sat and I played the song. I could see the awe on both of their faces. When the song ended I asked, "Is there anything needed in the song?" I realized that there was no response. "Viper", however, screamed, swore and shouted to play the song from the top again. I played the song from the top again. At the end of the song, I could hear subtle noises of weeping coming from the corner where Aziza was sitting. I was not sure, because Aziza turned and backed me with her hands covering her face. I asked Aziza if she was crying. She wept even louder and just said in Bajan dialect "dah real sweet hear!" 'Viper" did look a bit emotional as well, but was able to control his emotions. I knew at that point that this was the song to beat. The songs: "One People, One Nation" and "People Respect Yourself" – both I arranged and produced, won the national calypso crown. Below are photos of Aziza with her prestigious trophy and with me, after I spotted her in a fast food restaurant, days after her big win in 2016.

*2016 Barbados Calypso Monarch, 21-year old Aziza Clarke with Arranger/Producer, Ricky Brathwaite.*

Nevertheless, equally rewarding of wins came in 2019. Calypsonian "Classic" (William) contacted me via mobile phone and asked if he could come and chat with me. I responded in the affirmative and we arranged a convenient time to meet. "Classic" arrived at my studio and asked that I listened to the song he wrote for the year's Calypso Competition. I listened and was not totally impressed. "Classic" started to explain to me that he was aware that the song was a very simple one but was difficult to write. He then explained the concept to me and asked that I listened again with this explanation in mind. I listened again more critically and understood the concept. He asked if I was keen on working with him on it, because he did not want any other arranger to work on it. I agreed but recognized that it would require me to pull out all the arranging techniques necessary. I asked "Classic" to record a rough vocal track and began to work on it almost immediately. Days after, I emailed him what I done thus far, and he loved it. I thought… well if he likes the rough version, we should be in good shape when the song is completed. The song: "One Song" was in response to a new system where the two-song tradition was reduced to calypsonians singing only one song in the competition.

"Classic" did win the crown and was in contact with me through the entire process: from studio, to rehearsals, to props. This is what made it special. Ordinarily, once the production is completed, there is no more contact between the artist/writer and producer.

"Classic" even sourced ideal passes to attend the event for my wife and me. He also requested via WhatsApp that should he win he would like me to be on stage with him. The below photo and WhatsApp message represent that occasion.

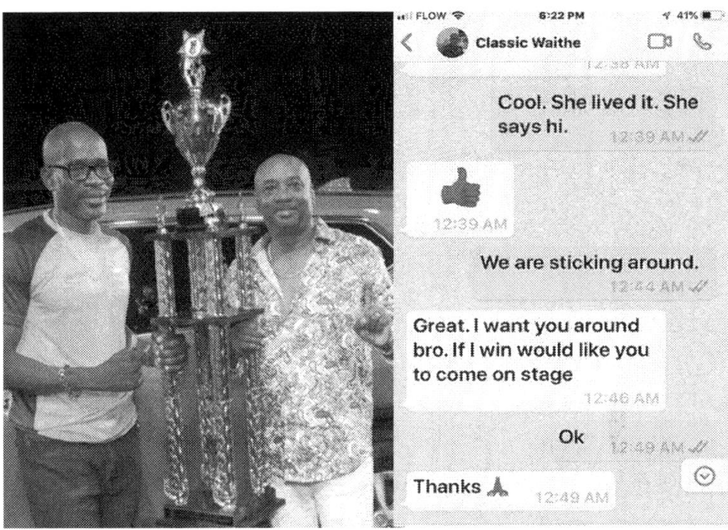


*2019 Calypso Monarch of Barbados with Arranger/Producer, Dr. Ricky Brathwaite.*

Another special memory was when I was invited to be a founder member of the inaugural West Indian Jazz Band. This was really, special, because I always believed that if the Caribbean could come together utilizing all of its strengths, the rest of the world would have to sit up and take note.

It would be remiss of me if I did not mention how St. Lucian, Luther Francois was probably instrumental in rekindling my career as a trumpet player before the West Indian Big Band stint.

Luther had visited Barbados with the main purpose of laying the music bed for a Caribbean movie soundtrack. He called me up and asked if I could play trumpet on it. I was embarrassed, because I had not seen the trumpet in quite a while. This was because sometime in the 1980s -- as earlier mentioned -- horn players and drummers were struggling to find work, because of the advent of modern technology: the drum machine and the synthesizer, in particular, that seemed to be replacing live players. I therefore gravitated towards the keyboards, which I played with several of my bands on the hotel circuit.

Once I communicated this to Luther, he became very angry and suggested I was crazy to put down the trumpet and that I was seen as the premier trumpeter in the Caribbean. He did not give up on me, but stated that he would be in Barbados for another two weeks. He urged me to find the trumpet and practice so I can play on the sound track. I did locate and cleaned up the trumpet, played on the soundtrack and this led to a number of significant gigs – The West Indian Jazz band being one of them.

# Chapter 10

## The Inaugural West Indies Jazz Band

Around 1988, I was invited by Luther Francois to be part of the inaugural West Indies Jazz Band. Luther had migrated to Martinique and aligned himself with the Martinique government. He was the brainchild of the idea of having the finest musicians from across the Caribbean culminate into one Caribbean melting pot performing only original compositions.

An airplane ticket was sent to me, along with a number of other carefully selected Bajan musicians. We met in Martinique and began rehearsing for two major shows. This was a great experience to have Anglophone and Francophone musicians from Martinique, Guadeloupe, St. Lucia and Barbados, play together, despite our cultural and language barriers. It felt like the genesis of something mega.

What was interesting to me was the level of musicianship emanating from the musicians from Martinique. The political and linguistic divide did not allow for this type of interaction previously. I later found out that the core of the band (rhythm section) comprised of members from the popular French orchestra, Malavoi. The composition of the West Indian Jazz Band was strings, guitars, electric bass, brass, percussion, backing vocals, and lead vocals. The arrangements from different musicians/arrangers in the band were interesting and challenging. I could not believe that simple 3/4 timing could present such a challenge. However, one thing that even transcended the music was the culture of Martinique. Before each rehearsal, each musician greeted all 30 members of the band individually with a kiss to the jaw. This was unusual for me. In the Anglophone Caribbean: good night or good day to all present sufficed. It literally took around 30 minutes before rehearsal started, because everyone entering the rehearsal room adopted the same routine of greeting and kissing everyone separately.

The government of Martinique was very professional and caring. They made sure that we were well fed, housed, and comfortable. Even if a member forgot a black pants at home, one was bought with no questions asked; neither was the cost deducted from one's pay packet. The two gigs were so successful that there was a strong consensus to repeat the entire process, with new and fresh arrangements at another time.

Because of this success, the group Malavoi invited the horn players: St. Lucian saxophonist, Luther Francois; St. Lucian trumpeter, Clarence Joseph; and myself on tour with them to Paris, France. I gladly accepted and we continued fresh rehearsals in

Martinique in preparation for Paris. I was totally blown away from watching the engineers and sound crew set up for the mega show at Zenith.

*The above photo is the touring band Malavoi. The top tier is the featured horn section. From left: 1st Trumpet, Ricky Brathwaite, 2nd Trumpet, the late, Clarence Joseph and Saxophone, Luther Francois.*

I had never seen such professionalism, stacks of speakers, giant mixing consoles and loads of stage equipment before this. I had only heard about and imagined such. We performed for about 40, 000 patrons standing and screaming in this huge venue called Zenith. They shouted, screamed, chanted, and sang along particularly with the songs with which they were familiar.

## Paris Hotel Room Saga

The morning after the gig – around 9:00 am, Luther and I were having a conversation about the event – the powerful moments, when we heard a faint knock on our hotel door. It was so faint that we were not sure if it was a knock or a noise from the adjacent room. Luther asked if I could investigate, since he was only clad in an under pants. I approached the door and asked if there was someone there. A male voice responded that it was the janitor. I peered through the peephole in the door. A man standing close to the hole waved his hand with a greeting smile and asked, in French, if I could open the door for a second, he just wanted to have a short talk with me. I cracked the door and was shocked by an army of police officers forcing themselves through the door in 'Swat' style, and indicating by the index finger-to his mouth gesture to keep quiet. All I was hoping for at this time was an explanation as to what was going on.

The police officers spoke to me in French and asked if there was anyone else present. Before I could respond, Luther exited his bedroom with his hands above his head and asked, in French, if there was a problem. The officers asked him to keep still while they looked around our rooms. I cannot remember any guns drawn. At this point, I became very angry, began to suggest that this was not right, that we were visitors, and should not be relegated to this type of treatment.

Luther kept warning me to relax, because those French police officers would kill me and think nothing of it. I obeyed. The officers then asked what brought us to Paris. Luther, responded, since he spoke more fluently in French than I did. The officers then apologized and stated that they were just following protocol. They left with smiles on their faces, and we had bigger smiles on ours. It was a scary scenario.

Discussions after the fact indicated that French police were very racist. I am not familiar with the culture, so I could only listen at the time and ask questions, hoping for legitimate answers.

# Chapter 11

## The Ring Bang Era

One day Gabby called me on the phone and asked if I could come up to Blue Wave Recording Studios, which is located is St. Philip, to the far south of the island. I had heard of Eddy Grant but had never met him, and did not know how to find Bayley's Plantation. It was suggested that I take a taxi and I would be refunded. So said, so done.

## Blue Wave Recording Studio

Once I got to Blue Wave Studios, I was met with a space that I had never experienced before. I had no time to officially meet Eddy, because I was quickly ushered into the performing room with the other three horn players: Michael "Smokey Roett, Cortez Callender and Lisle "Bimmie" Broome. I was not even given a few minutes to warm up. I could hear Eddy saying to Gabby, because the door connecting the control booth and performing room was still opened: "Gabberts, let's see how good he is now." The song being recorded was Gabby's 1985 hit, "Boots". This was a tremendous opportunity and learning curve for me. Eddy was very impressed with my performance, and even more so, my attitude. From then onward, I was privileged to play on just about every song coming out of Eddy Grant's Blue Wave Studios. This was the ringbang era.

## Working with Eddy Grant

Working with Eddy Grant created a special synergy; however, I thought I needed to spread my wings a bit. I felt stifled in a small environment where I had to constantly reinvent myself. I had won several awards as top musical arranger, top horn player from the Musicians and Entertainers Guild of Barbados [MEGOB]. At the peak of my career in Barbados as the number one trumpet player and top arranger, there seemed to be nowhere else to go within that small space. I decided to take a trip to New York to explore possibilities of earning a degree. I bought a return ticket to New York, without the knowledge of friends or family. I did not even have the slightest idea of where I would possibly stay. My then girlfriend, along with other musicians, who clearly did not support the seemingly uncertain move though that I was crazy.

Strange enough, the day before my scheduled trip to New York, Avonelle Connell, the sister of a friend, who I had known for many years, called me on the phone from New York to say hello. How suspicious this had appeared to my girlfriend Cheryl Carrington at the time. Avi, as she was affectionately called, agreed to pick me up at JFK International Airport. I stayed at her apartment, for a short while, making the ground my temporary sleeping space. The Living Room was completely carpeted, so a few added bed sheets felt quite comfortable.

# Chapter 12

## The 'Big Apple'

In inquiring about good colleges to attend, I was given several options. A Community College that constantly popped up on the radar was Kingsborough Community College. It was a newly built school, very spacious and was situated next to the beach.

I visited the school and on enquiring about enrollment procedures was told that I had to gain my SATs (Scholastic Aptitude Test) not withstanding any gains in London GCE (General Certificate in Education) certificates. I sat the exams in English and Mathematics and was assured a place in Kingsborough, pending registration and tuition fees. At this time, I was unaware that I required a F1 student visa in order to commence studying, and the school assumed I was an American resident/citizen.

## Divine Favor

New York residents paid half the tuition cost of students that were from out of state. In arriving to the pay window, I was told by the clerk that the fifty percent fee applied to me, even though I was, not only from out of state, but out of the country. I immediately stated that I was from Barbados and there must be an error somewhere. The clerk looked me full in the eyes and stated that she was sorry, but the roster reflected differently. She quickly summoned the next person in the line, as though she wanted no further discussion on the matter. Well… I thank the Almighty for his grace at that point.

My plan was to take my time and pursue my AA degree by skipping the spring semesters so I could continue to arrange music for the Barbados Crop Over season, as well as play in the Barbados Crop-Over Festival Band.

## The Barbados Crop-Over Festival Band

As the name suggests, I always believed that the band should not have been limited to the name Crop Over or Festival. The band, at that point, was the envy of the Caribbean -- a brilliant idea from a visionary, Elton Elombe Mottley, who was the then Director of Culture.

My thirteen years playing with the band were mostly enjoyable. Some of the finest musicians in the Caribbean were members of this band. The below photo of the band has been a continuous circulation on social media. Unfortunately, some members have migrated to a higher place.

*The Festival Band of 1987. Seated in the back from left: Bass, Former Chief Justice of Barbados, Sir Marston Gibson; Drums, David Burnett; Guitar, John Mathews; keyboards, Desmond Campbell; and Trumpet, the late Keith Ellis. Second row from back: Trombone, the late Anderson Griffith; Trumpet, Ricky Brathwaite; Trumpet, the late Shurland "Beans" Arthur; Trombone, the late, Lisle "Bimmie" Brooms; and Percussion, the late Vern "El Verno Del Congo" Best. Second row from front, from left: Baritone Sax, the late Issacs "Zackie" Holloway; and Michael "Smasher" Cadogan. Front row, from left: Tenor Sax, Cortez Callender; Tenor Sax, Jeffrey Grannum; Band Director, Michael "Smokey" Roett; Alto Sax, Andre Woodvine, and also on Alto Sax, Arturo Tappin.*

As earlier mentioned, the band was the cream of the crop of talented musicians. However, the band has always been viewed as a collective, relating only to Crop Over activities. There were several meetings with CEOs of the National Cultural Foundation on getting sponsorship for the band and having the band toured. There were other ideas of featuring the talent of the band in concerts, and even recording the band utilizing a mixture of original songs and calypso hits. To this day, all of these ideas have fallen on deaf ears or not seen as practical.

## Moving On

I would have been one of the mouthpieces for the band, which mainly comprised of members of the Royal Barbados Police Force Band. Year after year, musicians playing in the Festival band suffered some form of grievance, ranging from the lack of respect from the powers that be to issues at the main gate with not allowing one's spouse to enter through the same gate as the performers.

One year the committee of the Festival Band, of which I was a member, and the senior members of the Royal Barbados Force Band engaged in a special meeting. In that meeting, it was agreed that members of the Band would now be able to escort their spouses through the same gate as the musicians, but would require a special pass for backstage.

I drove up to the main gate with my fiancé, now my wife, and was told by security that my fiancé would have to get out and use another gate. I tried to explain that there was a recent agreement allowing one's spouse to enter through the same gate. Security insisted, regardless, that my fiancé get out immediately. No matter how I pleaded to call the CEO or some official of the National Cultural Foundation to have it cleared, it all fell on deaf ears. I, at the time, was blocking the gate from other members driving through. I explained that I was going to drive through the gate and park at the side to continue the conversation. As soon as I got into the venue and parked, a police officer grabbed my fiancé by the arm and proceeded to escort her outside of the compound. I was not aware of what was actually going on, because I got out of the car first, and was heading back to the gate to continue the conversation, while my fiancé was still sitting in the car.

An unknown patron alerted me that my wife was being arrested. I shouted in disgust and that alarmed a senior police officer who commanded the junior police officer to free my fiancé. There was no apology, but I presumed that there was some mix-up within the force and the senior police officer was not aware of the arrangement. This was only minutes before the start of the show.

Because of these on-going issues, a committee was selected to represent all band members. The committee, on which I was selected as a member, met on occasion to iron out a few pressing issues. Some of these issues were, band members having to stand in the same line as patrons to gain entry to the performance, guests of the band (spouses) having to use separate entrances and sourcing meals at intermission, where there is competition again with patrons to the shows. On some occasions, once food was sourced there was little or no time left for consumption, and the policy was, not to bring food on stage. Drinks were allowed. The individuals who were selected to adjudicate at the shows were treated with much more respect than the musicians were. They were escorted under tents and provided with food and drinks.

## The Straw That Broke the Camel's Back

Two years after these failed negotiations, I became very upset and decided I could no longer continue under the same system. The Festival Band committee was hopeful that after a subsequent special meeting some inroads, at least with respect to standing in long lines at intermission for food, had finally materialized. It was decided that food and drinks would be brought backstage to avoid the rushing around and late restarts. In 1989, during intermission there were no drinks or food backstage, as agreed, for the band. There were several angry phone calls to cultural officers and other officials, which did not seem to receive legitimate answers or adequate solutions.

That was the end of that chapter for me. I remained absolutely calm for the rest of the night's proceedings, even though I was extremely hungry. The others could tell that something was not right, but I decided not to have any conversation or discussion with anyone at this point. Enough was enough! I left the compound directly after the night's proceedings. Very early the next morning I dropped off my letter of resignation to the then CEO, Dr. Alison Leacock. The CEO made every effort to explain that she was new in the position and would assure me of taking the band to a new level. I explained to her that I was tired of the scant respect the band endured for many years and that was my time to exit.

Shortly after my exit, a few other prominent musicians took flight as well leaving a shell of what may have been a potential goldmine. I must admit though that my years playing with the band were very rewarding. The three trumpet players, especially, found much pleasure in playing with each other. We celebrated each other on technical stuff such as reading ability, tone, phrasing, and high notes -- nuances that would normally go unnoticed. In other words, it was a 'playground' for learning and developing and not only from the premise of backing artists. Directly after Crop Over it was back to school at Kingsborough Community College in the USA.

## Inspector Gordon Lovell

During one of my performances with the college band, I recognized that Inspector Gordon Lovell, who had retired from the Police Band and migrated to the USA, had also enrolled at Kingsborough Community College, and was a part of the stage band. I went over to him and re-introduced myself. He was elated, and we became study partners. I had dialogue with him and I was enlightened, through a series of questions, which revealed that I was studying illegally. I had studied for over a year without the appropriate F1 student visa. In fact, I was studying on a regular B1/B2 visitor's visa.

I called the US Immigration department to verify that this was true. I was told that I would have to stop studying immediately and acquire the correct visa, and that my actions were illegal. I was devastated and did not know where to turn.

The semester went by quickly and it was Crop-Over time again, and so I headed back to Barbados. During the festival, I communicated my visa issue to long-time friend Michael Richards (Aja). He hooked me up with the then US Ambassador, and the rest is history.

## The Brooklyn, NY Connection

Initially, my focus in migrating to the USA was to engage in academia. However, as word got around that there was this little guy from Barbados who plays a decent trumpet, I found myself in constant demand. I ended up performing and recording with some of the bigger names and pioneers in Caribbean music, names such as:

TRINIDAD & TOBAGO

- Sparrow
- Crazy
- Barron
- Roots Man
- Denese Plumber
- Singing Sandra
- Lord Nelson

- Sugar Aloes
- David Rudder
- Black Stalin
- Shadow
- Boogsie Sharpe
- Leston Paul – Arranger/Producer

JAMAICA

- Frankie PAUL
- Ernie Smith
- Fab 5

ST. VINCENT

- Beckett
- Frankie McIntosh
- Winston So So
- De Rebel Band

MONSERRAT

- Arrow,

and these names are by no means exhausted, but for the purpose of space, only the most recognized artists are mentioned.

I toured with Arrow for 5 consecutive years, while still a college student in New York.

## Arrow

Playing with Arrow allowed me to meet the 'who is who' in Caribbean entertainment. Trinidadian, arranger/producer, Leston Paul was one of those persons who valued my talent. He either got someone to call me, or called himself for dozens of studio gigs within the NY metropolitan area.

## King Hassan's Palace

One of my most memorable experiences was performing with "Arrow" and his multinational Force Band for the King of Morocco, King Hassan. About 500 musicians and dancers were ushered in from New York, Brazil and other countries for King Hassan's special birthday bash at his palace.

Special buses with tight security picked the performers up from the airport and transported us to the palace. Everyone was so fascinated from outside of the golden gates of the palace that cellphones emerged almost in harmony. At this point, however, the security, which could have been about 200 strong, boarded the buses with large guns and requested that all cellphones and cameras be placed in provided bags until further advised. This meant that we could not capture any of the activity that we all found so amazing and unusual. On entering the palace, it was noticeable how most people, although restricted to one particular area, constantly looked around almost uncontrollably.

During the show, I remember quite vividly that the men and women sat in different areas. All the men sat upstairs, and the king and the women downstairs. There were dozens of soldiers surrounding the palace who were vigilant of every move any member of the cast made. If one went to the bathroom, the door had to be left open. Not to mention that the toilet seats were of gold. The plates, cups and pillars keeping up the building were all made of 18-karat gold. It was like something directly out of a fairytale book. It was extremely depressing that we were not allowed to take photos, because all cameras and cellular phones were confiscated until departure. It was a once in a lifetime experience that I will always treasure, only for one hiccup.

## Disrespect from "Arrow"

When "Arrow" called me to ask if I could do the gig to Africa, I hesitated, because I had just bought a ticket for my fiancé – now my wife – to come up to New York to spend two weeks with me. The duration of the trip to Africa was one week. This was because there was only one flight out of Morocco per week, and the number of hours flying to get there was approximately 16 hours to and 16 hours back. I bargained with Arrow to pay me double the usual fee of US$1,000 plus the cost of the ticket, since my fiancé would now be seeing me for a mere week and would have to spend an entire week in a New York apartment by herself. I thought this was reasonable. Arrow, after some resistance, agreed to the adjusted fee.

## Payment

A day after the gig, there was a faint knock on my room door in Africa. I asked who was it, and the reply was "the boss." I indicated that the door was unlocked. Arrow entered with another member of the cast and very calmly asked: "Ricky, You want your money? Here it is." He folded the payment cheque as small as he could manage and threw it on my bed. I thought he was joking, because he left the room right away. I took the cheque and straightened it out to realize that it was a legitimate cheque with the correct date and his signature. I was deeply hurt. I took the cheque and pressed it out with a hot iron using a wet handkerchief. At that point, I knew I could not work with Arrow again, due to this scant respect, unless an apology followed. Two days after we got back to the USA, Arrow's manager called me asking if I was available to play at the Super Bowl in Canada. I bluntly turned it down. It was a painful decision, but one that had to be made.

Another memorable experience was performing with Arrow at the world famous Apollo Theatre for the 1991 Caribbean Music Awards.

The signage on the outside of the building alone, as shown in the photo above, was intimidating. I had been a fan of "Amateur Night at the Apollo" for years. This was the place where many stars were born. I recall that the audience was not an easy one to perform in front of. If they didn't liked you, you would know, and harshly so. Conversely, if they did appreciate you, they would let you know resoundingly. There was this little trumpet player from Barbados playing in such an iconic space.

I returned to Barbados after graduating college in 1993 and had not seen or heard from Arrow until about 25 years after when he called to invite me to tour with him again. He claimed he had missed his original trumpet player. He double-checked that he in fact, had all of my correct contact information. This however, never materialized, because he took ill, was confined to a wheelchair, and died less than a year after. Nevertheless, recording and touring with Arrow was a beautiful experience – one that I will always cherish, despite that one unfortunate experience. The Arrow experience taught me to appreciate other people's cultures and not to take anything in life for granted.

## Senior College

While a student at Kingsborough Community College, an older, white, male trombonist who was just sitting in with the jazz band asked if he could have a word with me. I agreed. His notion was that I could get a scholarship at any university or college in the USA. His exact words were "Any 4-year college in the States would lap you up." He gave me a direct telephone number to the Chairman of the Music Department at Long Island University, Bob Aquino, and suggested that I call just after 9 a.m. the following morning. I called, as suggested, and managed to secure an audition two days after.

## Audition

While warming up and waiting for the audition, a small Caucasian gentleman with the smallest glasses entered the room and asked if I was Ricky. I answered in the affirmative. We chatted for a brief moment and then he asked that I turn my back to the piano and try to identify the chords he was playing. He played four chords and I identified three of them correctly. He asked me to play the D Dorian scale two octaves. I thought…this must be divine intervention, because this was the only Dorian scale with which I was familiar. He seemed impressed and proceeded to play a string of chord progressions and requested that I improvise over them, without announcing what the chords were. Again, I chose the correct tonal center of C major and played constantly in the higher register. Bob Aquino took off his glasses, looked at me and in a warm tone of voice and quipped: "You are way above college level." I was not sure what he meant by that, but decided not to respond. He then asked where I was from. Once I responded that I was from Barbados, he questioned where in Jamaica was Barbados, followed by where I got my formal training.

## Scholarship

After some explanations and sharing of information, I was offered a half-scholarship. I was extremely excited. I was told to go home and think about it and let him know if I was accepting it. When I got home and worked out the half-scholarship, it meant that I would still have to pay the other half of US$60,000.00. I became very depressed and wondered from where I would get that sort of money. My roommate, Avanelle Connell suggested that I call back and turn down the offer, since it seemed out of reach.

I allowed two days to go by while I weighed all options. On the third day, as I was about to call Mr. Aquino, the phone rang. I answered the phone and it was Mr. Aquino on the other line. I indicated that I was just about to call him. He insisted that I speak first then. Something deep down inside of me prompted me to allow him to go first. He announced that there was a department meeting and the half-scholarship was upgraded to a full 4-year scholarship. My hand suddenly went numb and my voice disappeared as well. Mr. Aquino kept asking …"Ricky, Are you there?" Suddenly my voice reappeared and I expressed gratitude and thanks for the confidence in me. He urged me to pick up the confirmation letter at my convenience and return the acceptance form with some degree of alacrity.

## Life At LIU

*Source: LIU, Brooklyn Campus, 1991*

## Scholarship or Performing Gig?

About one week after registering to attend LIU in the Fall of 1991, I received a call from Trinidadian guitarist, Jeff Medina – the now guitarist with the legendary band The Commodores – I still don't know how he found me in a vast metropolitan area like New York, and he never told me. Jeff told me that he had recommended me for a

Big Band gig in Catskill, Upstate, New York that backs all the big artists passing through, such as Stevie Wonder, Dionne Warwick and others, and to expect a call from the agent. He said in his Trini-New Yorker accent "Rick, think about it man! It's a good gig". I said ok, and thanked him for thinking of me.

A few days later, a gentleman called and asked if I knew Jeff Medina. He went on to say that once Jeff Medina recommended me for the gig he did not even want to audition me, all I had to do was to agree and he would put everything in place for me to join the Musicians' Union and take care of all the paper work. One question that I remembered him asking, which I thought was a strange one, was if I attended Berkeley School of Music. I responded quickly: no, sorry, I attend LIU." He responded very quickly after saying, "Good. They all sound alike." I did not respond, and so he continued stating what the gig entailed etc. The gig was actually paying US$1,200 per week, and he wanted a decision in one week.

## Hard Choice

I could not sleep at night thinking about the fact that I had just accepted a full 4-year scholarship to a credible private University, and to turn it down might result in never being able to secure another one in the United States of America.

My roommate, Avanelle Connell came to me on regular intervals asking if I had made my decision. I asked her what she would have done if she were in my predicament. She empathized with me admitting that it was a tough decision, but urged me to continue school, that a scholarship was difficult to secure. She thought that other similar opportunities would present themselves, since I was a great player. I slept on her advice and by the next day, I was clear in my mind that I could not forfeit the scholarship.

Before the week was up the agent called me back to find out my decision. When I told him that I could not accept the gig and why, he sounded rather puzzled. He actually tried to convince me that gigs of that nature were rear and difficult to acquire. I became even more confused, but thought that I should make a clear decision and stick to it regardless. We both exited the conversation feeling a sense of loss.

I started school at LIU in the Fall of 1991. Essentially, LIU was more of a medical school with a fantastic music programme. Because of the nature of the school, I was forced to engage in many of the sciences such as Biology, Physics, Chemistry, in addition to a host of other academic courses. The BA degree leaned more towards teaching and education, but presented a good balance of jazz performance, jazz theory and arranging.

## Tragedy Strikes

At that time, I lived on Rockaway Parkway, Brooklyn, which was predominantly a white neighborhood. As earlier mentioned, I shared an apartment with a Barbadian beauty, Avonelle Connell, who had been living in Brooklyn for many years. I had met her in Barbados through her British sister Donna Connell, who I met many years prior, at the age of 16 years old.

The apartment only had one bedroom, which Avi shared with her six-year-old son. I therefore slept on the ground, which was well carpeted and augmented with a few bed sheets. I felt a little uncomfortable, because Avi did not have a male friend and was sending cues to me on a daily basis, to the point of frustrating herself because I showed no interest.

I thought the best thing to do was to find another place to live and so I moved to Flatbush Avenue – an area of lesser status, with a longtime girlfriend of my mother's. This time I had my own bedroom, even though I was told that I should get my own telephone line installed as well, which I did.

One night, Avanelle Connell invited me to accompany her, just for the ride, to pick up her son Shawn. I had a Biology examination the following day, and had to refuse the trip. That night she met her untimely death. Apparently, her mechanic allowed her to use his car while he worked on hers. On her way to the mechanic after she had picked up her son Shawn, an unknown man jumped on to the car's bonnet and sprayed the car with bullets – one penetrating her lungs. Her son, who seldom listened, did listen this time around and took refuge behind the passenger's seat. This eventually spared his life. I still, to this day, wonder if I had accepted her invitation, if she would be alive today or both of us killed instead. It took me a long time to accept her death, because I constantly reflected on the many conversations we shared together, including her looking forward to saving enough money to return to Barbados and opening her own business. Every day she would vent her frustration by literally dumping her day's 'garbage' on me. That was also tough on me, because after a long day at school I just wanted to relax, and this was difficult to do in such a tensed environment. Anyway, school was always my focus, and I was determined not to be distracted by anything else.

## Commuting to School

Brooklyn has a fantastic train and bus service that allows one to get around quite effectively without a vehicle. I however had to take a bus and two trains daily in order to get from home to LIU, and back.

Long Island University was where I met and performed with a number of internationally known musicians. World renown, Spike Lee taught in the Film department. I was fortunate to perform as lead trumpeter in master classes with American jazz greats like saxophonist, Joe Henderson; trumpeters, Freddy Hubbard and Jon Faddis and Jimmy Owens – the latter two being my private lessons trumpet tutors.

# Chapter 13

---

## Performing with USA International greats

## Trumpeter, Jon Faddis

One day the deputy chairman of the music department, Pete Yellen, called me into his office and announced that Jon Faddis was invited to conduct a master class at the school. He wanted to warn me in advance that Jon Faddis could be a difficult person to get along with, and since I was the lead player in the band, it was highly probable that he would pick on me. So said, so done.

During the performance, Jon Faddis was positioned in front of the band without a microphone, while I sat in the band with a microphone in front of me. During the song, there was a high section for the lead trumpet, notes above high C. As I began to play my part,

I was astonished that Faddis played an octave above me. It sounded as though someone was whistling. In amazement, I immediately stopped playing and just stared at him, with a look of unbelief. Faddis stopped the band, in front of an audience of about 300 persons, including my then fiancé, Debbie, who was sitting in the front row. He looked directly at me and aggressively asked, "Why did you stop playing man?" I was so ashamed that I had no idea how to respond. He continued, in front of the audience: …"Are you from the Caribbean?" I think the sun has done something to your brain." The other band members did not find it funny. They all kept straight faces, while there was an instant chuckle or two from the audience.

After a while, he recognized that I did not find the whole thing intriguing and urged me not to stop again, because he was depending on me to stay in tune at that high register. I had never heard anyone play that high before – at least not in a live setting.

After the concert/master class, to add insult to injury, Faddis came over to me. I was standing next to my fiancé who was holding my trumpet. He rudely suggested to me that I should never allow a female to carry my trumpet. He then proceeded to invite her to accompany him to the Hilton Hotel where he was staying, and suggested that everybody deserves a better life. Debbie scolded him as disrespectful, acknowledged that she was not an American, and we both walked off. As we exited the school compound, Faddis, in his sleek red car, summoned me over. I hesitated, but Debbie urged me to go over and see what he wanted. He immediately apologized for his behavior, offered to give me free private lessons, and jokingly added that he would even work on the one 'lock' located behind my head. This broke the tension a bit. He eventually gave me his phone number in New Jersey and I did a few classes with him at no cost to me or the school.

## Saxophonist, Joe Henderson

In another master class at LIU Joe Henderson, with his very quiet and unassuming demeanor, invited me to the play with him to the front of the band. He stopped the band at one point and equipped, "Ricky, go for those high notes with conviction – hit or miss." I went for the high notes with authority and without fear of missing. Joe looked back at me and nodded his head in acknowledgement. After the concert, a young woman, identifying herself as from the Press, came over to me and interviewed me for a newspaper of which I cannot recall. She, in her comments to me suggested that she saw the way Joe looked at me, and she believed that he was impressed with me.

During the interview, Joe came over to me, interrupted the interview and suggested to me that I call Queens College of the City University of New York, ask to speak with the Chairman of the music department, and say to him that Joe Henderson asked you to call. "I am going to recommend you for a music scholarship," said Joe. I did as Joe asked. The Chairman responded quite forcefully, but in an authoritative voice, that once Joe Henderson recommended me, there was no need for an audition. I had now manufactured an unnecessary dilemma. There were a few things worth considering: the distance to Queens College, as well as the fact that I had signed an agreement to attend LIU. Joe obviously was unaware that I had already secured a scholarship to LIU and I felt very comfortable there.

I had not heard about Joe Henderson prior to the master class, but found out subsequently that he was arguably the greatest tenor sax player alive. In fact, in 1992 celebrated American trumpeter, Freddy Hubbard gave me a free ticket to Carnegie Hall to what was billed as a clash between Freddie Hubbard and Joe Henderson. It was a brilliant night, but the major newspapers, the following day, were all in favor of Joe Henderson as the winner of the battle for the night. I actually agreed with the Newspapers. Joe Henderson played the most complicated 'licks' and demonstrated a great command of harmonic knowledge that was superior to what anyone else in the band or Freddie demonstrated that night.

## The Brooklyn Experience

While living and going to school in Brooklyn I played with several bands. I enjoyed playing with an all-white Big Band called The Towns Men Orchestra. The band comprised of about 20 members. I played 3rd trumpet next to some of the finest trumpeters that could be compared with the best in the world. I do not recall being paid more than U.S.$75 per gig, but I learned how to phrase and interpret Big Band jazz over the three year period with the band.

The soca band I enjoyed playing with the most was a Vincentian band called D'Rebel Band. Understanding the nuances required in performing the soca genre, must be heavily credited to this band. In addition to the music, I do not recall one quarrel among band members in my five years of performing at many functions with the band. Everyone knew their roles, regardless of one's musical ability, qualifications or experience. The band was very popular throughout the USA and travelled around the USA and Canada backing some of the finest in reggae and soca music: the likes of "Sparrow"; "Crazy"; "Gabby" and many others.

There were two interesting and memorable occurrences performing with the band that are worthy of mention. In 1992, the band was booked to travel from New York to St. Vincent, for one week, to perform for their annual carnival season. We did play at other smaller gigs. However, the night's performance in the park, which was labeled "Clash of the bands", was sort of an unpleasant one. The MC, a popular Barbadian announcer, Win Callender made his way on stage to loud booing from the large crowd. I was not sure what that was all about. Then when the MC announced that I was on lead trumpet and from Barbados, I was also booed. Meanwhile, some band members in the rhythm section were whispering to me not to worry. It was a difficult pill to swallow, because I had never experienced this kind of hostility before. The booing did not last very long, although it felt like eternity. It did affect my performance for the rest of the night.

Anyway, the show and band's performance were well accepted. After the show, I was told, that the Vincy people did not like foreign intrusion, and not to take it personally. That did massage my ego a bit. The entire trip was an enjoyable one, regardless.

The second strange occurrence was when the band made another trip, this time by bus, to Toronto, Canada to perform at a popular ski resort. The band, as usual, was well received. However, on returning to the United States, the bus was stopped at the border and checked for legitimacy. All persons were asked to disembark. Some persons were allowed back on the bus, including me. After thirty minutes, a few key members of the band were not allowed to get back on the bus. In fact, about five of the band members were eventually deported back to St. Vincent. I was not clear at the time what the issues were. I found out later that those members were awaiting particular documentation and were not allowed to travel until the process was completed. It was one of the saddest days of my life. I cried for days, because the band and members that I become so fond of was no more.

New York, despite the unusual crime, loud sirens and blatant racism, was the place to be. The space alone was a learning curve. Racism was not so bad in New York until I travelled to Houston, Texas to do a gig. An entourage of musicians travelled from New York in several private cars to perform in Texas for a mothers' day concert. The backing band, again, was D' Rebel Band. The cream of the crop in Trinidad artist were on the card, including Trinidadians Shadow and Black Stalin, who were present in the car I was travelling in. I had no idea that Shadow was so funny. He cracked Jokes from the time we left New York until we reached Texas. There was joke on top of joke. Before I could properly digest one joke, another one followed. At one point, my stomach started to hurt from all of the jokes – and excellent ones.

However, this was all marred for me when we reached Texas. We stopped by a small mini mart to grab some snacks to eat. We all got out and headed to the mini mart, because we still had another thirty to forty five minutes' drive before we reached the performance venue. When I got to the white female cashier to pay for my snacks, I realized that she did not look to happy. Why? I had no idea. She took long to engage the convey belt, even though there was no one ahead of me. I thought I would slide the snacks closer to her, in an attempt to assist her. She gave me a stern look followed by… "What are you doing?" I responded by saying that I was merely assisting. She literally shouted… "I don't need no help." The biggest error was my response of "I'm so sorry darling." This was a normal Caribbean expression. For her, it was taboo. She exclaimed, under her breath…"darling?" With that, she gasped, as though she wanted to vomit and quickly recused herself from the cash register. I was confused, because I had never experienced such rejection in all of my travelling experiences. Shadow must have heard or seen what entailed, and came over to the unattended cash register in order to defuse the situation. He calmly suggested that he would pay for everybody's snacks. About two minutes after another female cashier dashed over to the cash register, replacing the original one while apologizing for the original cashier, claiming that she had taken ill. That ordeal consumed the musicians and artists in the car for the rest of the journey. The conversations were centered on the racism in the South, which I was very ignorant of at the time. In fact, I was invited to perform back in Texas only months after, but declined.

Another group that I played with in New York and enjoyed performing with was a Pop/R&B band called, Latest Report.

## Latest Report Band

This group was very versatile with members from the USA, Barbados, Belize and Trinidad. The band performed R&B, soca, reggae and a small percentage of smooth jazz.

## Spice & Co.

Playing with the pre-dominantly 'white' Bajan band, Spice in the 1990s was an eye-opener from a number of fronts.

Founding members of the band were: Alan Shepherd on keyboards and lead vocals, Dean Straker on rhythm guitar and backing vocals and Roger Foster on bass. Spice became extremely popular performing reggae, calypso and pop with a South African feel.

After a while, the group added backing vocals: Tamar Marshall and Jan Gibson to the lineup; and later a three-man horn section: Ricky Brathwaite, trumpet; Michael Richards (AJA), trombone and Cortez Callender, saxophone.

The band was extremely professional. One thing that stood out in my mind was the fact that one was unable to detect if there were personality issues within the band. Unlike the black Bajan musicians, a drummer or guitarist did not pick down their instrument at rehearsal and quit over a simple misunderstanding. I have seen a situation where two band members got into a heated argument on a drum roll coming the wrong place, but those disagreements were quickly resolved for the larger task at hand. Rehearsals started on time, and if there was a time set to finish, that was also honored. I was never privy to any name bashing either at rehearsal or during a performance. These were some of the main differences that I observed while playing with the band, Spice. I put it down to a learning experience.

I have also played with Emile Straker in his Party People band, and again, there was joke after joke, before one could recover from the first one, but never "loose" and degrading gossip chat that is so evident within the black contemporary bands.

## Tek 6 – The Band

The name for the band Tek 6 emerged out of a need to produce a vocal group that was on par with those of the American vocal group, Take 5. Because the band was characteristically Bajan in nature, with the exception of one Caucasian Canadian vocalist, I thought that the name of the band should reflect Bajan culture through a word that is constantly used in Barbados [tek], meaning to take.

*The members of the band from left to right were: band leader/trumpeter/keyboardist and vocals, Ricky Brathwaite; the late André Grosvenor, lead vocals; wife, Sue Grosvenor, lead vocals; Bass/lead vocals, Winston "Socks" Welch and Lloyd Denny, guitar and vocals.*

The band practiced in St. Peter, Barbados at the home of the guitarist, Lloyd Denny. The vocal component of the band was excellent. This was the most significant feature of the band and became the selling point, even though all members were quite efficient on their instruments. We played a couple of gigs and were well received by the public. We were in the process of recording with the intention of hitting the road, touring the Caribbean and North America. However, there was one element that continuously showed its ugly head.

The lead vocalist, André became overly protective of his wife Sue. A simple correction of her intonation or harmony, created an aggressive response from him, even if the corrections were done with the kindest of tone and carefulness. This aggressiveness from André became a nuisance. Replacing him would have meant replacing both lead vocalists. This created the demise of the group. Band members really appreciated having the racial diversity of the group, which eventually would prove difficult to retain. The demise of the group was painful for me. It seemed as though striving for excellence was a constant burden.

I created several groups with different purposes in mind, but the mentioned groups were the ones that gave me tremendous satisfaction. Most groups broke up because of a dire lack of purpose from some band members, who did not appear to have the ability to see beyond 166 square miles of limited space. Again, I would have had several opportunities to live abroad, but always felt that I had some special calling in Barbados, even though I could never quite put my finger on it. Meanwhile, I always found myself having to kick down unnecessary barriers in my pursuit of excellence.

## Studio Gigs

I was also fortunate to work in several music-recording studios in New York, with many top-level arrangers, producers, musicians and engineers.

The arrangers/producers that left an indelible imprint on my life were Trinidadian, arranger/producer/musician, Leston Paul and Vincentian, arranger/producer/musician, Frankie McIntosh. The way they approached music was nothing short of genius. Leston Paul allowed me to play trumpet on a great number of soca songs from established artists coming out of Trinidad and Tobago, around the period 1988 – 1994.

## NY Studio Dispute: "Ricky this is calypso, yuh know!"

I recall most vividly being called to the Platinum Recording Studio on Fulton Avenue, New York to engage in a recording session with Trinidadian, calypsonian, "Crazy" (Edward Ayoung). On my arrival, I recognized that there were a few players whom I had not met before. Trinidadian trumpeter, Errol Ince was one of them. I introduced myself, warmed up and sat where I saw the trumpet chart positioned on the music stand. I did not realize that there were two separate charts: 1st and 2nd trumpet. I was aggressively told by Errol that I was sitting in his chair. I shifted to the next chair immediately with an apology. Leston spoke from the control booth to the performing booth asking if the horns were ready to go. The song was 1994 "Paul Yuh Mudda Cum" by "Crazy". We did, what is referred to as a 'dry run' to ensure there were no issues in the charts and everyone was comfortable. Halfway through the 'dry run' Errol stopped the horn section and questioned me on my feel for the music. He shouted, again, aggressively in his raw T & T accent: "Ricky, this is calypso yuh know!" My first response and questions to him were: "What am I playing? Am I playing spooge?" Initially, I was a bit confused. However, it quickly dawned on me that the written phrasing on the score might not have been interpreted in a way that would be aesthetically determined as 'Trini' in style or interpretation. That was really a learning curve for me; but, living in New York, generally, was a learning curve. Anyway, we got through the song. It sounded very nice, and turned out to be a hit. Errol and I eventually became very respectful of each other and became friends.

## Graduating from LIU

After graduating from LIU in 1993 with a Bachelor's Degree in Liberal Arts and Jazz Music, I was recommended for a scholarship at Colombia University by Dr. Gloria Cooper – one of my lecturers at Kingsborough Community College. I was subsequently contacted by Columbia University and offered a 2/3 scholarship with the proviso that I would teach free for the other part – 1/3.

I accepted with the provision that I begin in the fall of 1994 after a period of rest in Barbados. However, once I got to Barbados, I was inundated with several job offers that were difficult to turn down, since I wanted to be close to my to-be-wife, Debbie.

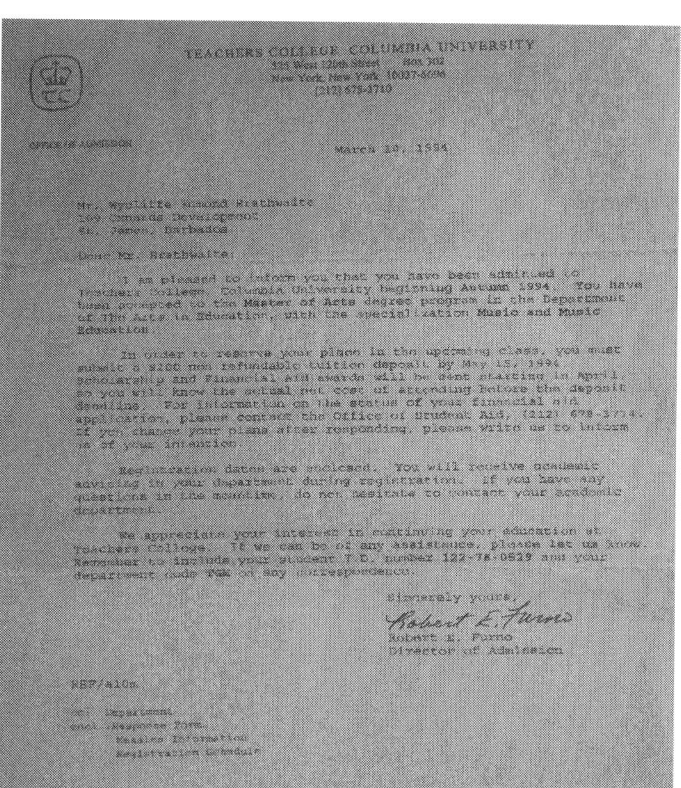

TEACHERS COLLEGE COLUMBIA UNIVERSITY
525 West 120th Street Box 302
New York, New York 10027-6696
(212) 678-3710

OFFICE OF ADMISSION

March 1[illegible], 1994

Mr. Wycliffe [illegible] Brathwaite
109 [illegible] Development
St. James, Barbados

Dear Mr. Brathwaite:

I am pleased to inform you that you have been admitted to Teachers College, Columbia University beginning Autumn 1994. You have been accepted to the **Master of Arts** degree program in the Department of The Arts in Education, with the specialization **Music and Music Education**.

In order to reserve your place in the upcoming class, you must submit a $100 non refundable tuition deposit by May 15, 1994. Scholarship and Financial Aid awards will be sent starting in April, so you will know the actual net cost of attending before the deposit deadline. For information on the status of your financial aid application, please contact the Office of Student Aid, (212) 678-3714. If you change your plans after responding, please write us to inform us of your intention.

Registration dates are enclosed. You will receive academic advising in your department during registration. If you have any questions in the meantime, do not hesitate to contact your academic department.

We appreciate your interest in continuing your education at Teachers College. If we can be of any assistance, please let us know. Remember to include your student I.D. number 122-78-0529 and your department code TGM on any correspondence.

Sincerely yours,

Robert E. Furno

Robert E. Furno
Director of Admission

REF/[illegible]

cc: Department
encl.: Response Form
Measles Information
Registration Schedule

# Chapter 14

## Family Life

Family has always been important to me. This cannot be trivialized. While studying in the USA, I returned home on vacation and met my beautiful wife Debbie. We got married on July 6, 2000 on board the cruise liner "Fascination", as shown in the below photo.

**Debbie**

I met Debbie at a concert in Barbados when she was 20 years old. A mutual friend, Andrea King, introduced us and we immediately gravitated towards each other like a magnet. Prior to that formal introduction, I would admire Debbie walking through Bridgetown at a particular time on evenings. I would drive through Broad Street, around that time on occasion just to admire how pretty she was and how briskly she walked to wherever she was going. I especially noted that she would always be alone. I knew she worked in Bridgetown, but not where. So, on introduction, it felt like I had known her years before. We talked a bit while the three of us walked around the stadium, but extended the conversation on the phone when we got to our separate homes. In fact, both Andrea and Debbie asked for a ride home, because they shared an apartment then.

As soon as I reached home, I did not hesitate to telephone Debbie. That first telephone call lasted for approximately six straight hours – from 11p.m. that night to about 5a.m. the following morning. Every time we tried to terminate the conversation, another topic would emerge extending the talk time by another hour. In fact, there was one occasion where we talked on the phone for about eight hours, where Debbie only had enough time to take a shower, without eating breakfast, before heading out to work.

I had asked Debbie her age while at the concert, but she did not ask me for mine, at least not at the function where we met. I was always careful to keep the conversations in a trajectory that would avoid the topic. I was home, in Barbados, for a three-week break from school in the USA. In fact, I was preparing to head back to New York in five days, and was hoping she did not ask my age before I departed. We, however, seemed to be getting closer and closer with each conversation.

The following day I picked Debbie up from her home in my hired car and headed off to the beach, which became a daily routine. We had so much fun that we stayed at the beach until sundown. On driving her back to her home one evening, she finally quietly suggested… "I told you my age, but you did not tell me yours." I thought…oh boy, this might be the end of a short, beautiful relationship. At that point, I thought it might not be a great idea to reveal the truth. Another voice suggested that I should tell the truth, despite the outcome. I said softly… 'Oh…I am 32 years old." I can still see the look on her face. She paused, took a short breath and asked… "Are you serious?" I responded immediately in the affirmative. Debbie looked amazed and suggested in plain words that I was very old, and she had never dated anybody that old. She continued: "but you don't look so old." I asked her how old she thought I was. Her response was, about 25 years old. It did not turn out the way I had anticipated. Debbie actually complimented me on how good I looked for my age, and even questioned what food I was consuming to look so good. She would bring up the age issue several occasions after, either on the fact that she has never seen herself dating an older man or reconfirmation on how good she thought I looked for my age. Anyway, our days of dating, having fun, long phone chats and falling in love, went by very quickly, and it was time for me to head back to college in Brooklyn, New York.

Debbie accompanied me to the airport for my departure back to New York amongst many tears from both parties. Before I entered the departure lounge, Debbie made it clear that I must call her as soon as I reached home in New York. I did that and called her back in Barbados as soon as I reached my apartment. That conversation, which was supposed to be a brief one, lasted for over an hour. In the 1990s, long distance calls were very expensive. My monthly telephone bill, thereafter, was around US$400. No matter how we discussed the phone bill cost and the need to curb it, we found it difficult to stick to strict time-periods.

The fact that we are now together for over thirty years and married for twenty-four, suggests that it was all worth it. The age difference of twelve years does not feel as drastic as when we first met. As the saying goes: the generational gap narrows as the relationship grows. Unnecessary disputes and quarrels that once consumed our relationship, after marriage, have also narrowed.

## Myles and Saniya

The union produced two lovely children: Myles, now 23 years old and Saniya, now 17 years old – both graduates of Harrison College and committed to the performing Arts.

Myles, the more reserved of the two, is an adept piano player, who also plays the trumpet, ukulele, Harp and a few other instruments.

Saniya is a classically trained dancer and actress and sings as well. She is a 2016 NIFCA silver award-winning medalist for her mixed-disciplined piece of dance, drama and singing entitled "I Know Who I Am".

*Myles 11, Saniya 5 (2012) St. Gabriel's & Harrison College*

Myles and Saniya are now both very involved in the Arts. Myles is a classical and pop/jazz pianist attaining up to Grade 6 Practical and Theory from The Royal School of Music, London.

*Harrison College, Dec. 9, 2018, and Graduation, July 6, 2019, respectively.*

Saniya has acquired up to Grade 5 in Ballet and Modern dance through the British Dance Examiners ISTD. In 2016 she won a mixed disciplined silver medal in the Barbados National Independence of Creative Arts [NIFCA] and has played a leading role in several dance presentations in her short life span. She played the lead acting role as Efi Nkono in the NCF's 2017 Crop Over Heritage Bus Tour and was a part of the silver award winning team

***NIFCA** (National Independence of Creative Arts – Barbados) Silver Medalist. Mixed discipline Performance piece – "I know who I am" [November 2016].*

Saniya released her first CD single – "My Hopes and Dreams" at the tender age of nine years old. The song was written and composed by Saniya and her father Ricky Brathwaite, who also arranged and produced the R & B/Reggae track:

Debbie, my wife of 24 years, is not interested in being involved in the performing arts. Her passion is in Marketing and has been working in this field for many years. However, she is extremely supportive of her family's passion for the arts. When I produce a song, I always let her hear it before it is finalized as she is quite capable of hearing when the lead vocal is sharp or flat, if the bass is not sitting well with the track. I refer to her as my unofficial co-producer.

## Karate Life

While working at Rediffusion Services Ltd., a doctor was brought in to do an evaluation on the wellbeing of the staff. Most of the staff was much older than I was. At first, I thought… I don't need that. I decided, regardless, to step into the room where the doctor and his tools were located.

The procedure was a slight stick on the first finger inducing a small bit of blood. That blood was then placed on a gage to test if one's cholesterol was normal. From my recollection, there were four color-coded stages. I can recall quite vividly, though, that any color higher than orange, as communicated by the doctor, was threading on dangerous ground. To the doctor's surprise, my level was just under red. The doctor looked at me with an alarming facial expression and equipped: …"Ricky, watch it boy!" He instructed me to get more tests done right away.

It caught me by surprise, even though I was definitely eating too many fried liver-cutters and soda drinks, almost on a nightly basis. He asked me if I was involved in any form of exercise, to which my response was, no. He further instructed me to devise a serious exercise plan, as from the following day.

It so happened that I attended a health expo the following day, as instructed, and saw a large group of people all dressed in white costumes, moving very slowly, and in sync. It was called Tai Chi. I liked how it looked. I enrolled and started practicing that same week. Even though I saw some benefits almost instantaneously, Tai Chi got boring after only one year of practice. I then joined the Barbados Shotokan Karate Club. In three years, I earned the rank of Shodan (Black belt). I liked it very much, because people were always around to encourage and motivate me to keep training. I ended up acquiring five black belts (go dan). Because of the stringent exercises three days a week, my blood pressure and cholesterol levels became normal.

The below photo shows me as a sensei (teacher) instructing a class of only junior black belts.

Karate was not only beneficial physically, but mentally as well. Having five black belts also instilled a kind of discipline at that level that would be very difficult to explain. I am certain that this form of discipline transcended all odds and was at the root of me completing my doctorate, which was certainly no brush over. Even though I have not trained for over ten years, my mental health has remained stable because of the past stringent training.

# Chapter 15

## Paint It Jazz 1997

While working at Rediffusion Services Ltd., now Starcom Network Inc., I received a call from the organizer of the Barbados Jazz Festival Gilbert Rowe. He asked if I would be interested in performing at the 1997 Barbados Jazz Festival. He said that he would like me to play at Farley Hill in St. Peter, Barbados. I quickly responded that I was not interested in Farley Hill. I thought I would struggle, as a trumpet player, in such a vast open space venue. I also thought that since the Barbadian public had not heard me play in such a long time, I would prefer to be a headliner, rather than just a supporting act. I had also witnessed world-renowned trumpeter, Wynton Marsalis literally struggle to engage the crowd at a previous

Barbados Jazz festival. My feeling is that the crowd was not welcoming to straight ahead or bebop jazz. I did not want to suffer a similar fate in front of my hometown folks. Gilbert immediately said he would call me back in ten minutes and hung up the phone. In about five minutes, he called back and said he would put me to open for Patti LaBelle at the Wildey Gymnasium. I graciously accepted.

My initial idea was to play rearranged jazz standards. I was however nervous, because Patti Labelle is known as an R&B/Pop artist, and the patrons attending would really be coming to see her. In other words, playing the kind of repertoire I initially had in mind might not have been the most practical choice.

## Sound Check & Performance

I was given a time by the organizers for my band, which comprised of the late Ricky Aimey, bass; the late Adrian Clarke, piano; Terry Arthur, pan; David Burnett, drums and Ricky Brathwaite on trumpet and flugelhorn, to sound check. What was quite disturbing was, an hour before the band was scheduled to perform, Patti Labelle's band was still sound checking. The band waited and waited. By this time, the doors were opened and patrons started to arrive. Therefore, my band did not get a proper sound check. From the first note to the end of the approximately 45 minute performance, members of the band could not hear each other and the bass distorted the entire performance. Nevertheless, patrons loved the performance, which culminated into a standing ovation. International icon Roberta Flack, who was sitting in the front row with her Barbadian boyfriend, "Ziggy", subsequently said on local radio that trumpeter, Ricky Brathwaite was excellent, and she expected great things to follow.

## Wynton Marsalis

About two years after, Wynton Marsalis was again a Headliner, playing in the same venue. I attended the event. Wynton seemed to have adjusted his repertoire to include a few more popular standards and interesting arrangements, unlike his previous performance, that warmed the patrons' hearts. At the end of the night's performance as I was about to leave the facility, I saw the organizer of the show waving to me in the audience, while Wynton hastily made his way from the stage to the backstage area. I was not sure if Gilbert was waving to me, because of our fallout two years prior. He however, made his way over to where I was sitting shouting, "Wynton wants to meet you." I was in awe. I thought…meet me?

My wife and I were facilitated to the VIP section and then to the backstage area where I was able to meet my favorite trumpet player and took the above picture with him.

This picture meant so much to me that I have framed it and positioned it conspicuously on the wall of my recording studio. There was no politics involved in this. Politics in Barbados, as a small island state has infiltrated just about every aspect of life. This was a very short discussion with Wynton, as he asked if I intended migrating to another space that is more Arts-focused. I responded in short "one day."

At one point when I was starting to take the many soundbites of advice to depart Barbados a bit more seriously, I again, thought about my country and how I might be able to make an even greater contribution. A call from the then Prime Minister of Barbados, the Hon. David Thompson, shelved once more that thought of migration.

## Party Monarch Musical Director/Band Leader

In 2008, Barbados saw a change in government from the Barbados Labour Party, (BLP) to The Democratic Labour Party, (DLP). I was always labeled as a DLP supporter, even though there is no real evidence to support this claim. However, I was approached by the then Chairman of the NCF Board, Ken Knight. He asked if I would be interested in taking over as the Party Monarch Band, Musical Director/Band Leader. I was not aware of the associated politics but requested a couple of days to consider it. I discussed it with my wife who did not believe I should accept it, because it did not align with the direction and trajectory in terms of the path I was pursuing.

One day after requesting time to fully consider the position, I received a call from a journalist of the main Barbadian Newspaper -- Nation Newspaper. He said he was calling to do an article on me because he was informed that I was taking over the direction of the Party Monarch Band from current bandleader, Adrian "Boo" Husbands. I was in shock. I explained that I had made it absolutely clear that I would have to think about it. My first inclination was to call the NCF and announce that I was not interested in the position. In further conversation with the journalist, I was enlightened that the removal of "Boo" Husbands from the position was due to his support of the losing party (BLP). I wanted nothing of it, I explained. I am not sure if my sentiments travelled back to the powers that be, but I received an unusual call from the then Prime Minister of Barbados, Mr. David Thompson. He stressed that the reason why I was chosen for the position was because of my brilliance that had too long been stifled, in addition, he had just taken over the government and did not want any hiccups. Well…it was difficult to reject the Prime Minister of Barbados, so I accepted the position.

From the first day of rehearsals with the band, I could strongly feel the resentment of some of the older band members towards me. I had made up my mind that I was going to groom one of my trumpet students, who played next to me, for the position. I knew I could not continue for more than two years. I think my attitude towards leading the band showed clearly and the response from some band members was reciprocal.

Things got better as the first year progressed. From the second year, I could not understand what had transpired. The resentment got progressively worse. By this time, Prime Minister David Thompson had fallen ill to cancer. This was not motivational at all. I however, made a call to the Chairman requesting permission to make changes to the band. I thought that the clientele and type of music the gig required merited a younger set of faces in the band. I thought that the Barbados Community College was turning out a crop of talented players that were better suited. Some of the older members, while excellent players did not read musical notation and were putting a strain on the time in which the job could be done. In addition, I had always felt that the best persons for a particular gig were never engaged, but had a problem with the same faces constantly surfacing at the compromise of the broader culture. In other words, some musicians found it difficult to survive because of the existing political climate.

Eventually, those same older musicians in the band and their connections with the political powers that be engineered a way in having me removed as Director of the band. I received a letter from the NCF informing me that my services were no longer needed. This did not come as a shock, because rumors were circulating rampantly.

## Government Minister's Intervention

The day after I received my letter of termination, Government Minister, Donville Inniss, who is also my neighbor, rang my doorbell and asked if he could buy two of my CDs. I immediately analyzed that his visit had nothing to do with the purchase of CDs. I went into the studio, collected two CDs and gave them to him as complimentary. He then took this opportunity to question me on the termination of my position as Band Director. I explained the full story to him. He then invited me to his house the same night, revealed that a few ministers would attend and suggested that I bring the letter of termination with me.

I hesitantly attended the political party at Minister Inniss' house that night around 9 p.m. As soon as I arrived, I was greeted by Minister Inniss, who walked directly over to a group of persons, which included Prime Minister Freundel Stuart. Mr. Inniss summoned me over and introduced me to Prime Minister Stuart. He further prompted me to explain the situation to Prime Minister Stuart. I was very uncomfortable and embarrassed, because I did not know the other gentlemen in the group, and was not accustomed to these types of political-typc social events.

Minister Innis also suggested that I show Prime Minister, Stuart the termination letter, which I did. Minister Stuart quickly read the letter and seemingly became annoyed. I am not sure if the Prime Minister had indulged in the drinking of alcohol, but he began to literally shout, "These people at the NCF are lost. I will be calling the

NCF early tomorrow morning and deal with this." This attracted the attention of other persons at the event that were not in close proximity. I politely excused myself and walked over to my house.

The following morning around 6 a.m., I called Mr. Inniss and indicated that I was no longer interested in the position and would be happy if he would contact Prime Minister Stuart to communicate my sentiments accordingly. Minister Inniss insisted that I let the Prime Minister deal with the problem. I insisted that I had made up my mind and was quite happy if it did not go any further. He said he respected my decision, and the rest is history. I can remember, quite vividly, those days when there was no political interference in matters related to entertainment. This was when entertainers made very little pay in plying their craft. Once the possibility of musicians generating money through connections to politicians became a reality, there was visible manipulation, and this eliminated much of the fun and creativity that once existed. Culture in Barbados, with entertainment as a driving force, continues to be heavily politicized. Entertainers are now divided into political letters of B or D. Political interference is in every facet of Barbadians' lives. It has now been shaped into a science. From the perspective of the performing and visual arts, it has benefited some while others have been noticeably maligned.

I can remember the NCF commissioning me as Musical Director of the Cohoblopot Band. This I was engaged in for three consecutive years. I have always been appalled that the same musicians are involved in every show and event. I therefore sought to expose and give other musicians a chance to put food on their tables as well. I hired two white musicians to play in the band, who would not generally be associated with such events. The band was extremely tight and had good and diverse visuals. During the sound check for the night's performance, two top officials approached me and enquired as to who were all of those white people in the band. I bit my tongue and decided not to respond. The blatant display of disrespect for the white musicians of the Barbadian community, who have always been contributory to the Bajan soundscape, was appalling.

Since Barbados, under any dispensation, continues to be a place of 'political tribalism' in order to survive, I was forced to channel my skills, talents and knowledge outside of the country that I love so dearly. After all, The University of The West Indies being in the top 5 percent of universities in the world does develop global citizens. I was therefore forced to come to the realization that if opportunities are scarce in Barbados, there are always other options – sometimes, forced options. I arranged horns for bands all over the world. I trained trumpet players that came to Barbados specifically to study with me. I networked with other musicians across the Globe.

Politics and the struggles to make a real meaningful contribution in the Arts convinced me that if I were not going to migrate to another country then I would have to embark on a new course and trajectory. Management was that natural chosen path.

# Chapter 16

## Corporate Management Life

I got an unusual call from Mrs. Margarita Estwick, General Manager of the record company, West Indies Record Limited [WIRL], which had a large Caribbean music portfolio. There is tremendous history of WIRL and its significance in the development of music in the Caribbean. I was asked if I would be interested in working at the company.

On accepting the job, I recognized that there were political issues that needed to be addressed with some degree of alacrity. One of those pressing issue was, some artists, not having good material, but because of their popularity, constantly found a place on the yearly artists' compilations. I received calls in abundance from artists. This marginalized newer artists and other artists who had great material. I knew this would have been controversial, based on the fact, that it was not only the norm, but involved very close political connections as well.

Second, artists complained feverishly of the meager royalty payments they received from time to time. My determination to make WIRL a viable and respected institution created some tension. The sales team summoned me one day to a meeting. Their main concern was not seeing the same more popular names on the jacket covers of the compilations, which could affect their sales. I gladly met with them. I assure them that I was auditioning good and commercial material not popular artists, who did not have good material. Of course, they disagreed with me an asserted that this was not the status quo. I realized that WIRL had been operating for over twenty-five years on a hit-or-miss basis. There was no clear plan. Practically, most of the sales representatives admonished me in clear terms that they were not sure if I knew what I was doing. I, however, explained to them that this was why WIRL compilations were not successful in the past and they needed to trust me. The meeting ended on a high note. I auditioned all of the cassette tapes sent in to 'WIRL' and distributed what I thought to be good songs to credible studios and engineers at the time. This created a new paradigm, and they all did fantastic productions. When the two compilations were completed: "Soca Gone Wild" (volume 1 and 2) I decided to release them much earlier than normal. Volume 1 contained the faster songs, now known as 'power soca'; while volume 2 was more in the ragga soca direction, now known as 'sweet soca'. Once the compilations hit the radio stations there was an immediate buzz, not only within the company, but the radio stations and across Barbados.

In fact, the cassette plant had never produced at that volume in years. It couldn't handle the heavy requests and constantly broke down. I remember the sales team was finally happy. In fact, a few members of the sales team would approach me, either in my office or somewhere on the compound to congratulate me on a job well done after all. A few of them even apologized for being so initially abrasive.

This was not the only unpopular decision that I made or agitated for. Every year, before I became the Production Director of WIRL, I had noted that as part of the marketing strategy, a few things were not prudent to me. A band was assembled, a venue secured, and the artists (Calypsonians) were asked to perform the songs on the WIRL compilations. In my opinion, it was always more of a a disaster. The artists, because the songs were new originals, had challenges with remembering the lyrics and forms of the songs. This was cascaded to the band, which suffer similar challenges; because if the artists were unsure of the songs, the band would be as well.

I had a meeting with the marketing manager, Ms. Kay McConney, who was an excellent marketing person, but was new to the business of music, and still feeling her way around. I was able to convince her that the regular album launch featuring the artists/calypsonians, backed by a band, needed to be revised, and why, as aforementioned. I advised that the large sound system should remain in place to provide a clean and big sound at the yearly venue, which was the then popular nightclub "After dark". It was appropriate at the time, not only because of its popularity, but also because of its spacious indoor and outdoor aesthetic. We had the artists/calypsonians who were featured on the albums attend the launch, but not to perform as in the past, but to autograph album jackets and engage in speeches, if necessary. It was an astounding success, and to my mind, the first time this was done. This fresh and experimental idea resonated; and was adopted by many persons engaging in CD/Album launches, which continues to the present.

## The Demise of 'WIRL'

I worked at WIRL for just over one year, until the building was mysteriously gutted by fire. I remember turning up for work the Monday morning to see part of the building gutted by fire and the entire staff in regular clothes, some standing and crying in disbelief, and others trying to assist where possible. No one informed me of the happening. I was the only person in formal working attire. My office was eventually relocated to the cassette plant, which was directly across the yard on the other side of the compound, while a section of the main plant, which remained partially intact, continued business on a smaller scale.

A few months following the fire there were rumors of the company being sold, but no direct communication was received from Barbados Shipping and Trading (BS&T), the major shareholder of the company. In fact, one day while I was at home on my lunch break, preparing to head back to work, I received a call from one of my staff asking if I had planned to return to work that day. I thought… that was a strange question. I was informed that the desk, computer and chairs that were in my new office had been removed and only four walls remained. I thought this must be some prank. When I got back to work and headed to my office, the door was left open so I could see from a distance that the room was empty. Seconds after, a Director of Barbados Shipping and Trading (BS&T) approached me without any explanation and softly asked if I had any keys or credit cards belonging to the company. My response was a cold, no. I looked at the Director in amazement and without a word, exited the compound. There was no explanation, no dialogue, or letter – nothing. A day later, the managing director of WIRL – another senior member of BS&T, Mr. Philip Corbin, telephoned me to apologize for the situation and wanted to know if I would like to be repositioned in another management position somewhere in the company. I did not even have to give much thought to the question. I immediately turned it down. When asked if I was sure, my response was, “very sure.” It was one of the most disrespectful and embarrassing moments of my career. In fact, I vowed that I would never work for Barbados Shipping and Trading (BS&T) again, even if it were at the level of CEO.

## Rediffusion Services Ltd.

Shortly after that terrible ordeal, I was contacted by the then Programme Manager of Rediffusion Services Ltd., (now Starcom Network Inc.) David Ellis, who asked if I would be interested in supervising the music and DJs working on their three stations: Voice of Barbados [VOB], Yess Fm and the Caribbean's lone cable radio station [Rediffusion]. This was indeed a new dynamic for me, in that the three radio stations had three totally different formats and the job required a sound knowledge of various types of music, including the latest hit charts, as well as 'oldie goldies'. This I knew would be a challenge, but was not difficult to achieve once I put in the time and research.

The Managing Director, Victor Fernandes and Programme Director, David Ellis introduced me to the brilliant DJs and announcers at the time: Dennis Johnson, KB Kleen (Kevin Hinds), Admiral Nelson (Anthony Nelson), Nirmal Thani, Gregston Sealy, Patrick Gallop, Christine Bourne, and Cassandra Samuels. They all had different and contrasting personalities, but were quite pleasant to work with.

I introduced or re-introduced a playlist system where DJs or announcers had to prepare the music they intended to play before hand and submit a copy of their play list to me before going on air for vetting. This allowed me to vet and monitor the stations to ensure that the three stations stuck to their demographics. There were times when DJs deviated from the playlist, but I did not worry too much once the sound of the particular station remained intact. Of course, some DJs or announcers got memos if they deliberately flouted policy. Some DJs forgot at times that even if I were not physically in the office, I still had access to what transpired on air from anywhere on the planet. In addition, I always kept a copy of their playlists with me at all times.

It should be noted that while engaging in these diverse transitions relating to management and performance, my commitment to sharing knowledge had always been present. In fact, Barbados Community College has always been the medium to do so.

## Barbados Community College

After some time studying in the USA, I returned to Barbados in 1994 and realized that there was no music programme on the curriculum at Barbados Community College. I boldly wrote to the Barbados Community College Board and explained, in harsh terms, that this was unacceptable.

One day while taking a casual drive and in casual attire on my way back home, I got a call from an anonymous caller. It was the principal, Mrs. Norma Holder, asking if I could attend a Board meeting in about 20 minutes. I explained that I was not appropriately dressed for any Board meeting. She insisted that I come anyway, that the Board members would understand. I arrived at Barbados Community College feeling totally out of place. I walked a bit subdued into the Principal's office. The secretary smiled and told me to hold on three minutes that the Board was expecting me, and she would escort me over to the Boardroom. On my arrival to the Boardroom, I began to apologize without hesitation. The Board members seemed very understanding and even joked around a bit. This gave me a bit of comfort. My academic transcripts were thoroughly perused, the music ones in particular. The Principal then questioned me on the possibility of creating a range of three-month certificate courses in areas such as: arranging, choral writing, jazz improvisation and computer music. I gladly accepted, and those courses ran from one month after the mandate for approximately three years. I still cherish the simple, sweet gesture in the form of a plaque, as shown below, presented to me by my 14 students, then, congratulating me on my performance as opening act for international icon, Patti Labelle at the then, 1997 Barbados Jazz Festival. My performance at the Jazz Festival may have paved the way for my smooth entrance through the doors of Almond Resorts Inc. as a senior manager.

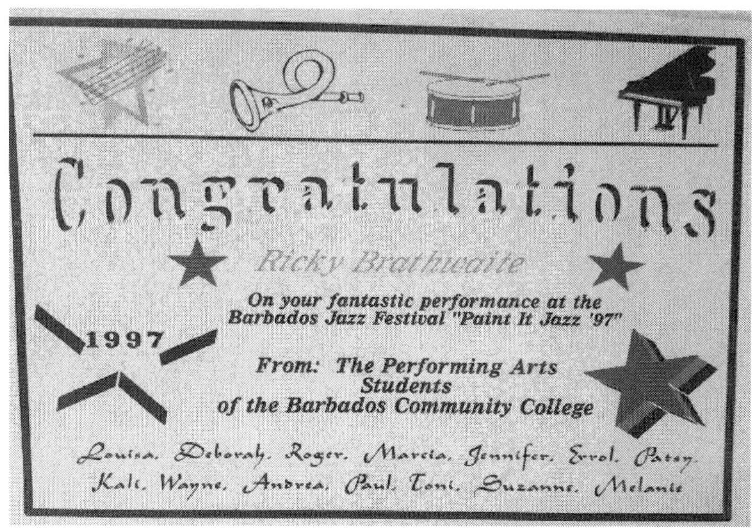

## Almond Resorts Inc.

In 1998, Mr. Ralph Taylor, Chairman and Managing Director of Almond Resorts requested to meet with me. This was to discuss the possibility of introducing international quality entertainment through the setting up of a new Entertainment Department with full time musicians, dancers, sound and lighting engineers and DJs. I was still a member of the management team at Redifussion Services Ltd. I was quite comfortable there, working closely with the Disc Jockeys and announcers, but thought I was under-utilized. After meeting with Ralph Taylor, I felt that this new venture was a challenge I was willing to undertake. Mr. Taylor gave me a mandate of fully executing the new and innovative program in three months. I hired a full-time staff of 30 entertainers: musicians, dancers, sound and lighting engineers, in addition to two disc jockeys for the hotel's Rachel's Night Club. No hotel chain, to my mind, in the entire region, had ever undertaken such a bold venture.

This venture proved to be considerably more cost effective and successful than hiring nightly entertainment. Of course, this affected other entertainers that were not fortunate to be on the Almond monthly payroll. I was, months later, further mandated to create a carbon copy of the same Barbados entertainment system in St. Lucia. I was promoted from Entertainment Manager to the new position of Director of Entertainment. Twenty-one entertainers, including musicians, dancers and sound and lighting engineers were hired. Between the two hotels in Barbados - Almond Beach Village and

Almond Beach Club and Almond Morgan Bay of St. Lucia, there was now a grand total of fifty-one full-time entertainers. My personal preferences were the dancers from St. Lucia, but the band from Barbados. The below Nation News Paper clipping shows a few band members who attended the band's new CD launch at the, then, Almond Beach Club in Holetown, Barbados.

18 FRIDAY, OCTOBER 6, 2006.

Groove

MEMBERS of the Almond Band with their new CD. At end of the line is entertainment director of Almond, Ricky Brathwaite. At right, Callender Girl chats with DJ Admiral Nelson and wife as A&B Music boss Norman Barrow and Almond communications director Doug Hoyte listen in.

(Pictures by Charlie Pitt-Grant.)

## CUBA

Ralph Taylor, to my mind, was, and is a visionary. He was the vision behind having an Entertainment department that was particular to Almond Resorts Inc. He proved the critics to be totally wrong. Having a unique entertainment department allowed for the control of quality nightly entertainment. As a result, the surveys on the quality of entertainment between all hotels rose considerably. Because of

Taylor's commitment to quality, he thought I should go to Cuba in search of fresh ideas for Almond's entertainment. Taylor intercepted, through his good office, and curbed a few obstacles orchestrated to ensure that the trip to Cuba would fail.

Going to Cuba at the time, as recommended, meant not being present at home for my wife's birthday. Taylor granted me the permission to travel with my wife and, then, 2 year-old son, Myles. Of course, I did not want to burden the company with unnecessary bills, so I opted to pay for their trips, and did.

On reaching the hotel, which was pre-booked from Barbados, we were told that no children were allowed in the prestigious Cuban hotel. We were a bit depressed because the hotel was immaculate. The staff was too. So excellent was the staff that they recommended another hotel that would allow children that was not 5-star, but just below – 4-star. I could not imagine what the 5-star was like, because the 4-star was great.

The first show we attended the following night was much closer to the new hotel. The show is said to be the largest and most popular throughout Cuba called "Tropicana". Below, is a photo with my wife and me, backing, along with Cuban spectators observing the spectacular night's performance.

The show comprised of about fifty dancers with spectacular costumes. I did not think the dancing was amazing, because it consisted of more coordinated walking than dancing. I supposed the costumes were too cumbersome to engage in any technical dance routines, but demonstrated what a spectacular show represented. It was very enjoyable and rewarding. It also gave me a new perspective that I was able to communicate to my senior dancers, and have implemented a few days after.

One thing that has stuck with me, as a senior manager at Almond Resorts Inc., was confirmation that classism in Barbados does exist. My nature as a human being was never one that puts individuals in particular categories. If my spirit for an individual does not gel, I avoid that person. I remember hugging a gardener on an occasion. In fact, it was a regular occurrence for me to hug staff members who were labeled to be at the lower end of the spectrum. I guess I was being monitored for some time. One morning I was walking across the Almond hotel yard, in route to my office. A senior Human Resources manager approached me and walked beside me in the same direction. I was cautioned that there was some discussion among other senior members that I was too familiar with junior members of staff, and that I needed to draw a clear line between subordinates and myself.

I had heard similar sentiments when I sat with my entertainment staff at general staff meetings, rather than at the head table or management designated spaces. This did not deter me from speaking or hugging subordinates in public. I always saw everyone as human beings, and this translated into having little or no sick leave in my department. In fact, I was assertive and forceful as a senior manager, yet my staff felt comfortable approaching me on matters relating to work, and even personal matters. To my surprise, this was also noted by internationally acclaimed Harry Belafonte, in his observation of my relationship with my staff and guests alike. I was not even aware of his presence at the resort.

## Harry Belafonte

One afternoon, my boss, Ralph Taylor told me he was having lunch in the Horizon restaurant with a real international superstar. I enquired, with a chuckle, who would that be. It was Harry Belafonte. Ralph quipped… "Ricky, I'm sure his conversation is going to be centered on music. I don't know anything about music, other than I have a CD player and CDs in my house." We both laughed, and I thought, Harry Belafonte? Of course! The three of us sat together for lunch for about one hour. Strange enough, the conversation was more about his lovely hotel suit and his love for Barbados and its beautiful habitants. He also mentioned how he was impressed with the way I interacted with the entertainers and guests.

At one point, Harry Belafonte suddenly turned his chair to me, in a sudden switch of topic. He asked if I could help him recall an older Jamaican reggae singer whose name he failed to recall at the time. He thought the Jamaican singer was brilliant. I had hired and brought in Jamaican artist, Ernie Smith for the millennium celebration, so his name immediately came to mind. As soon as I mentioned his name, Harry shouted in his husky voice: "Yes… there you go!" He then asked if there was way any he could get in contact with Ernie. I asked to be excused while I headed off to my office in search of the CD – one that Ernie Smith had autographed and given to me as a souvenir. The CD had all of Ernie Smith's contact information. The strange thing is that Harry Belafonte asked me if he could keep the CD, even though I indicated that the particular CD was available in the thrift shop a few yards away. Harry preferred the CD with Ernie's personal autograph to me. I quickly said to him… "Sure. No problem, Mr. Belafonte." Shortly after, I became visually disturbed, somewhere near the end of our lunch meeting. I casually asked Mr. Belafonte if he would be interested in treating the hotel guests to an impromptu 2-minute appearance that said night, as a part of the weekly cabaret show. I intimated that it was not a regular occurrence to have such an international legendary icon grace or shores, furthermore our hotel. I indicated that I was prepared to pay him whatever he charged for the performance. His response to me was "Rick, it would take all of the money you have in the Barbados treasury to pull that off." There was a short moment of silence, before rising to his feet and indicating, he would be heading back to his room until later on in the day. That episode bothered me to the extent that I was unsure of if I was out of place in asking, or if it was the manner in which I approached it. The Chairman, Ralph Taylor, thought there was nothing cynical about my asking, since it was my job as Director of Entertainment to provide the finest entertainment for our guests.

There was another episode of meeting an international superstar at Almond Beach Resorts Inc. This time it was Cuban Gooding Senior. Cuban actually approached me while I was walking over to the said restaurant – Horizon restaurant. With a big smile on his face, he said, "How are you? I heard you are in charge of all of the entertainment here." I responded in the affirmative. Cuban Gooding then asked if I knew who he was. I stared in his face, thinking he looked a bit like Cuban Gooding Jr. I thought, though, that it could not be, because he looked a bit older. I did ask if he was Cuban Gooding Jr. He responded in a stern voice… "No! His father." Anyway, we talked for a short while about what he and his son were currently engaged in, before heading off in different directions. We met again on about two other occasions, and had lunch together once.

He was always very funny and loved to engage in storytelling and jokes.

However, after 9 and a half years as Head of Entertainment, I thought it was time to recalibrate and refocus on my career as a performing and recording artist. I built a recording studio onto my house with just that paradigm shift of rebuilding my career in mind. I recorded my second CD album "Sunflower" and shortly after, my last CD "City Life" which I launched at the prestigious Frank Collymore Hall, in Barbados.

## Music Dilemma

After my personal productions and a few for other artists, it did not take me long after to realize that not much had changed on the Barbadian musical soundscape within the ten years that I had gone into artists and hotel management. Gigs were slow and artists did not rush to record with me as I had anticipated. My only other option was to pursue gigs and any other opportunities outside of the country. There was one major dilemma -- leaving my small closely-knit family to do so.

## Academic diversion

I decided, as a temporary measure, to produce a few promising artists while teaching at schools for a steady income. Ironically, one day Dr. Marcia Burrowes, the coordinator of the Cultural Studies

Programme at The University of The West Indies contacted me and asked if I would be interested in teaching a module within the programme. The rest is history, because I ended up becoming a student in the same Master's programme in 2010 and graduated in 2012 with a Master's degree in Cultural Studies. I decided that I might as well finish the academic process and went straight into research for a PhD. I completed the research in 2017 and successfully defended my thesis in June of 2018. I was awarded my Doctorate of Philosophy in Cultural Studies on September 28, 2018. My thesis interrogated areas of phrasing and interpretation, and how these nuances play out in unique ways between each Caribbean Island.

However, segueing from my Master's into PhD was a little more challenging than appeared at first glance. The reading assignments and information overload from my Master's took a toll on many of us. In fact, I had studied religiously for a midterm exam, having read and highlighted a bulk of the handouts, which would prevent me from re-reading all of this vast information. After a particular class, I left all of my organized labeled folders, temporarily, on my desk while I visited the bathroom. To my dismay and horror, when I returned to the classroom, all my folders were missing. In panic mode, I asked around – from security to faculty -- if anyone had any information on the whereabouts of this valuable information. Not one of the folders was ever recovered. I felt totally handicapped; this placed tremendous strain on my ability to function, and placed doubt on my ability to cope with upcoming exams. I was forced to devise a new strategy of study and retaining information. It also gave me a deeper sense of Faith and meaning in pursuit of the highest level of academic studies.

Getting to the level of Doctor was no easy task, but I cherish every moment of the journey. There were demons constantly trying to block my path, but through the grace of God, I was able to maneuver and navigate my way through the thick black smoke. While I give very little energy to many negativities surrounding my doctoral journey, there is one glaring one that is worthy of mention.

On the morning of my Viva at 9 a.m. on June 21, 2018, I experienced demons like I never had before. As part of my presentation, I had to demonstrate the Caribbean neo-soca direction that was en vogue. To do this, I secured the services of local drummer, James Lovell and bassist, Neil Newton. Thirty minutes before my presentation I got a call from James stating that he was caught up in traffic. PhD presentations are very formal and strict. Once the doors are closed, nobody is allowed to enter or depart. I prayed and prayed silently. Five minutes before start time, James showed up and set up his drums within 2 minutes. I thought ... thank you Lord, but the demons kept coming.

The technical people who had finished setting up and testing all of the equipment announced thirty seconds before the start of the presentation that the video player suddenly stopped working, and they were no other working ones on the campus. I was allowed fifteen minutes extra time to sort out the technical issues or have the Viva postponed to a few months later. At this time, I had become visibly upset and nervous. Just as the registrar was about to make the announcement, the bassist whispered in my ear that he had a portable video player in his bag. Neil was allowed to quickly set up his video player and was even allowed to operate it as well. The entire presentation was executed flawlessly, as though it was pre-rehearsed. Apart from being grilled for over an hour by my external examiner, Professor Paul Carr, broadcasting via Zoom from London, everything went just as well as the original plan.

Becoming a doctor was never part of my pursuit of excellence in a career in music. To say that I am elated to have reached this milestone in my life, would be a gross understatement. I was even more elated to have my family celebrate this profound occasion with me, as shown below.

*From left: Myles, Debbie, Saniya and Ricky*

It is not the 'norm' to give credit and to appreciate those persons who have contributed to one's success. It would be remiss of me if I did not make mention of the key persons who have guided me, advised me or proof-read my thesis in shaping it to a very high academic level

– one that would be realized long after it is logged in the annals of the University of The West Indies' libraries.

My main supervisor, Professor Curwen Best and Co-supervisor, Dr. Cleve Scott were the persons driving me to deliver the best version of myself. Professor Best left no stone unturned. Dr. Elisabeth Watson's contribution cannot be trivialized. She was the ultimate push to the finish line. Without her inviting me to her home for four consecutive days to trash out areas that needed clarification and rewording, the finish line would have been a bit further away. Even though I gave her a stipend of appreciation, she never once discussed compensation for her time and expertise throughout the entire time.

## Untimely Departure

It was painful that in just a few weeks after our meetings I received a WhatsApp message from her with what turned out to be her final request from me. She was adamant that she wanted me, and no one else, because she was not well, to assist her in delivering her lecture at the Barbados Museum, as reflected in the her WhatsApp message. (*R… meaning Ricky)

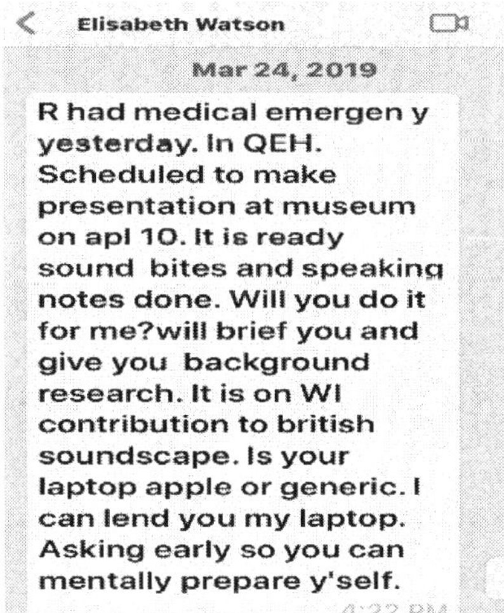

I agreed that I would do it. However, later that same day I received a call from the then coordinator of the Cultural Studies programme at The UWI, Dr. Marcia Burrowes, informing me that my friend and mentor, Dr. Elisabeth Watson had passed. I took it very hard, but accepted the fact that life was becoming more and more unpredictable, and very fragile.

Below is a photo of that lecture. Because Elisabeth's files could not be found, the content had to be altered and other participants added. The topic was "The Caribbean's Contribution to The British Soundscape". The participants were, from left: Dr. W. Ricky Brathwaite, Dr. John Hunte, Professor Evelyn O'Callaghan and Chairman, Dr. H. Stefan Walcott.

The Barbados Museum also brought back memories of a different kind when I was booked, some 10 years ago, as a featured performer. I recall being scheduled to perform with a then popular and exciting Trinidadian steel Pan group called Panazz, as shown in the below photo.

The band and I had engaged in a sound check the same day as the show, which ended rather late because of technical issues. When the sound check ended, it was just about two hours before show time. I made my way home and returned about thirty minutes after the scheduled start time for the show.

The most bizarre thing happened. As I arrived at the gate to the Museum and was being certified by security, I heard the Master of Ceremonies introduced me to appear on stage. I thought… I must be hearing wrong! Nobody checked to see that I had not yet arrived? Since when is one of the main headliners brought on so early in the show? I quickly indicated to security that I was just announced to perform, and I had to go. He understood and quickly cleared the path for me to make my way to the stage where the Trinidadian, Steel Pan group, Panazz was already in place and waiting for me to come on.

The strangest and funniest thing happened at home before making my way to the performance. I asked my wife to trim my moustache, but cautioned her not to take off too much, because it would have a negative impact on my trumpet performance. She seemed very meticulous, but I heard her sigh, "oh dear". I immediately asked what was wrong. She explained that in trying to balance the two segments of the moustache she accidentally brought one side too low and had to bring the other half in line with the other. At this point I was hoping for the best. When she said that she was finished. I looked in the mirror to realize that there was hardly any moustache left. All that remained was a line of hair representing a fraction of an inch. It looked so terrible that we both agreed it would be better to cut it all off. Anyone with a good understanding of playing the trumpet would know that the slightest adjustment to the moustache, a tooth extraction or a slight cut on the lips could hamper the best trumpet player's ability to perform at optimum level.

The group, Panazz was very dynamic. All members were versed in jazz improvisational techniques. The song I was asked to perform was "Feel So Good" by American, Trumpet/Flugelhorn player, Chuck Mangione.

I walked briskly onto the stage with my trumpet still in my gig bag. I took it out while talking to the audience about hearing my name announced while at the gate trying to get in. The audience laughed. I then indicated that because I did not get the chance to warm up I would have to do it on stage before I play. The audience and the band members laughed as well. I had to think quickly and use the mishap as part of the show.

I tried a quick warm up and discovered that I could hardly produce simple notes. Anyway, I remained as professional as possible explaining what the warmup was and why it was necessary, to more laughter, and even shouts from the audience. All that entered my mind at that point was the word, 'embarrassment'. It was very necessary to warm up if I were to get through this piece without mistakes. "Feel So Good" is a technical piece, which entailed a few high notes with little space to breath. Failure to hit them effectively and cleanly would ruin my reputation. After all, the song was a popular song that was frequently played on the radio. Even though I struggled a bit and had to utilize every bit of technical skill, it was very well received by the appreciative audience. After my performance, while walking to the backstage tent provided, I thought… things likc this would only happen in Barbados. International icon, Eddy Grant was in attendance. He and his entourage congratulated me and said they thought it was one of my best performances. I thought… well, why worry when the audience, along with Eddy Grant loved it.

## Matriculation

Ironically, after graduating from Long Island University (LIU) NY, in 1993, my focal point was always, how I may be of significant benefit to my country, Barbados. After earning my PhD in 2018, I had been given several pieces of advice, from prominent Barbadians on my course of direction. Some suggested that I leave Barbados and pursue becoming a professor. Others suggest that I look for a decent job outside of Barbados, because I would not gain the kind of respect of which I am deserving. One, then, Government Minister suggested that I leave Barbados and never look back.

I must admit that I was a bit confused over the numerous opinions and suggestions that came rapidly without a single request. Of course, I listened attentively to all of them and discussed them with my wife. I did receive offers with which I did not feel quite comfortable. My wife even got in contact with an agency of the Canadian Government who thought that I was exactly what the Canadian Government was in search of: musical experience, qualifications, talent etc. The consensus was that I easily qualified for the Canadian 35-point migration system. He even went on, trying to convince me, that once I completed and submitted all of the required documents and migrated to Canada, I would become a millionaire in less than one year. My mind, however, was firmly planted on sharing my knowledge, in a senior capacity that would benefit my country.

Soon after, the position for CEO of the National Cultural Foundation became available and one of the requirements advertised in the Nation Newspaper was a PhD in Cultural studies, as reflected in my 2018 doctoral graduation ceremony and PhD thesis, below. I applied and was interviewed for the position, but sadly, I was not successful. I thought… Rick, pick up the pieces and move on.

Just before my Graduation Ceremony of October 20, 2018, talk had already gone around that I was now a Doctor. It was initiated by one of my past band colleagues and PhD Cultural Studies candidate, who attended my Viva and posted the result to Facebook. This also triggered other social media postings by the late, legendary, Richard Stoute and others, as shown below.

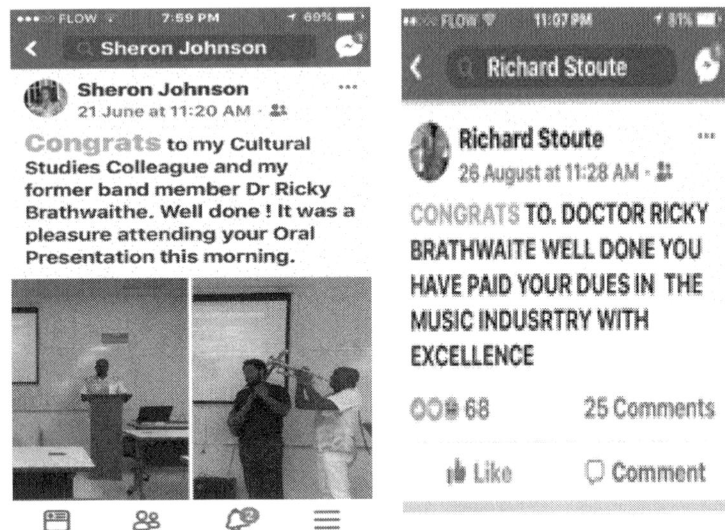


The Press wanted to get in on the action and contacted me requesting a story. I am not one who likes to be constantly in the media – social or print; however, I agreed to do the press release. The Press release triggered other calls from a few secondary schools requesting that I lend my expertise to the teaching system, especially in music.

# Chapter 17

## Secondary School Experience

Around the year 2018, I received a phone call, while hanging with my family at a popular mall in Barbados. This was a call on a Saturday afternoon from the Principal of one of our older and established secondary schools. During our short conversation, I was asked to hand deliver an application and resumé to the security guard at the gate, because I would be considered to teach music at the school. With some reservation, I decided to follow through on the request, since I was told that interviews would be starting from the following Monday.

I received a call from the school's Treasurer Secretary early that Monday, about 10:00 a.m., asking if I could attend an interview at 1:00 p.m. that same day. I agreed and started to prepare for the interview.

## Q.C. Boardroom

On being summoned to the Boardroom, after waiting for over an hour, I realized that the Treasurer-Secretary was quite aggressive in her manner of speech and body language towards me. I however, put it down to her natural disposition. I was not quite correct. I remembered that during the call from the principal days before, it was communicated that there was some politics going on where a past student was heavily favored for the job, but he (the Principal) would not be acceding to any novices at his school. Anyway, my resumé was interrogated by a few of the Board members. There was clear orchestrated aggression that made me feel a bit comfortable. To my surprise, the very principal who indicated that he wanted me to teach at the school buckled under pressure. He questioned my resume suggesting that it was very impressive and was intimidating – even for him as the Principal. At the end of the interview, the Chairperson thanked me for attending and declared that the interview went quite well.

I was not impressed with the questions nor behaviors of some of the Board members. In fact, I questioned, in my mind, how some of the said individuals were selected to be on the Board in the first instance. I also understood why the Principal was so adamant, initially, about having novices in his school. On hindsight, I also recalled him suggesting that there was too much politics at the school. However, after the interview, when I was asked to provide copies of my qualifications and other documents, I simply left the compound without doing such. At that point, I was clear in my mind that I wanted no part of the secondary school system.

## Harrison College

One year later, I was asked by the PTA Chairman of Harrison College, David Weatherhead, if I would be interested in undertaking the position of Trumpet Tutor for the school. I could not give him a definitive response at the time. In fact, there was some ambivalence on whether or not I should even consider it. The PTA President approached me again about two weeks later and this time added that he would really appreciate it if I could agree to do it, since he was trying to raise the standard at Harrison College in all areas. Since I was aware of his attention to detail, having played music with him for a number of years, I accepted the position. In the year 2024, I am still the Trumpet Teacher at the school and find it quite gratifying to be able to divulge and disseminate information to the future generation.

# Christ Church Foundation School

My commitment and teaching experience emanating from Harrison College, infiltrated into another secondary school. In April of 2020, the acting Principal of The Christ Church Foundation School, Mr. David McCarthy – past Deputy Principal of Harrison College, called me up and asked if I would be interested in teaching music at the school. The music teacher, Mr. Lowrey Worrell had undergone surgery and was at home recovering. As a result, first to fifth formers at the school had not engage in music for almost two months. My task would be to bring them up to the level where they should be. I accepted, and assured the Principal he had my 120% commitment.

I taught music at Christ Church Foundation for close to two months until Mr. Worrell returned to his substantive teaching post. Teaching at Christ Church Foundation School was not easy. Even to start the process was a bit of a challenge. The Principal said that it might not be necessary to go through the normal process and that he would speak to the Chairperson of the Board to avoid any further delay, as a matter of urgency. There was at least two days delay because a Board member tried to block the process, claiming that I was difficult to work with. If I had engaged with that individual five times in my entire existence, that would have been a lot, but this was just one example of living in a small myopic, socio-political society. I was again ready to recuse myself from the Barbados school system that seemed to be rooted in mediocrity and ignorance. However, because of the honest and candid conversation between the Principal and myself, I thought that I might be able to make a difference in my short tenure.

## Cultural Challenges

During my first week on the job, the Principal invited me to several functions and introduced me to the entire teaching body on all occasions. Most teachers welcomed me with open arms and respect. I found that the older teachers were the gems at the school. They reminded me of my days at school. They seemed caring and always willing to help. I could not say the same for the younger teachers – especially the females. This I would address later in this chapter.

My first class was first formers, 1Alpha 2. I introduced myself as Dr. Brathwaite, took the roster, told them a bit about myself and explained what I expected from them. Good behavior was one of them. Well, this was not the case for the first two weeks. There was much idle chatter, 'backchat' and the occasional fights. It seemed very much a part of the school culture. I had to, actually, beg students, at times, to stop talking, while I was talking as well as when I was not talking. Once I turned my back to write on the white board, the 'fish market' started. It was quite frustrating. I had to devise various strategies to gain their trust so that I could try to control the environment and bring some level of order to the classroom. In about the third week on the job I felt that they were not as restless as earlier times. They began to understand my style of teaching, and that there was no compromise in my standards. I too began to gravitate towards them and treated them as my own children. I even began to wonder what it would be like not to have them in my life at the end of my two-month stint.

## Observations

One thing that has stayed with me until this day is a 2$^{nd}$ form male student standing to his feet and saying to me; "Sir, we outsmart all the teachers at this school. They are not bright." I thought I would temporarily put music aside and engage the students further in discussions along this notion. I got to understand their mode of thinking, and partially where the line of demarcation stood between this generation and the previous one. One thing that I became clear on was that they desired to be heard and be allowed to express themselves, which might not necessarily be consistent with what transpired two decades earlier. As the children from, especially, forms 1 to 3 became more comfortable with me and my style of teaching, they became more vulnerable and divulged information that was astounding.

Just about every one of my second formers communicated to me that there were teachers who referred to them by derogative names.

By just looking around the class to the other 30 students, they, almost in harmony, shouted "That is true sir." They even identified the teachers who insulted them and referred to them by their names. I became visibly emotional at this point. I however, thought that since I was only a substitute teacher that I would not interfere with the current environment, and it would be wise to leave it in the state in which I found it. After all, I was already starting the job with the attached stigma of 'hard to work with'. As I worked feverously to focus on the syllabus, and what was required to bring different forms of students of different musical levels up to the requirements of the syllabus, I was also forced into the informal position of counselor.

In fact, when I announced that it was my last day at the school and the regular teacher would be back from the next school day, I could see tears settled in some of the students' eyes. I too started to choke up a bit while talking and I could tell that the students could detect it. As they had alluded to, and quite rightly so, they were smarter than given credit for. A lot of emphasis seemed to be placed on the older secondary schools, but I had witnessed the discrepancy.

Another episode that continues to be etched in my mind is a fight between two male third formers. One day during my third period, and strolling through the classroom isle, explaining a musical concept, I heard a loud thump. The students sitting in the font of the class rushed to the back where I was located. It was the sound of a punch from one student to the chest of another. It was quite scary, to tell the truth. I quickly directed all students to wait outside the classroom and asked the two boys to remain. They were all briefed during my first day of class that I was a 5th degree black belt in Shotokan Karate. I could detect that they had remembered that by the look on their faces. Since it was only 20 minutes short of recess, I went outside and requested that students collected their possessions from the classroom and they were free to leave for the day.

I went back into the classroom in seconds. The two boys immediately started to apologize, almost in unison, for their actions. I sat there with them for a while, even after the end of school for the day, counseling, and talking to them like any caring father would to his children. In the end, the boys apologized again, hugged each other and went their separate ways.

The news got around quite quickly. I was summoned to the office of the department head. I was asked to divulge of the events that transpired and instructed to submit a report to the Deputy Principal. I had promised the boys that the event would not be logged once they understood the gravity of their actions and showed genuine remorse. I communicated to the department head that the boys did not seem to be bad boys, but only needed the type of conversation and counseling that I offered them. I was, again told that the rules dictate that I file a report with the Deputy Principal.

I responded in the affirmative, but went over to the Principal's office and explained the different sides of the incident to him. I explained that the objective should not be to get the boys in trouble, because I strongly believe in my heart that my interaction with the boys was long lasting. The principal agreed with me and advised me to let it slide if I felt so strongly. There and then, I thought to myself that we tend to blow things out of proportion and are at times too bureaucratic.

I could tell that the Principal was appreciative of the mature way I was assisting in developing the students, especially the ones that had been literally written off by the system as rogues, dunces and failures of the system.

My last day of school, the Principal called me into his office and immediately stated, …"so much for the naysayers." I had not been familiar with the term. He then explained that he had only good reports from other teachers and students alike.

The Principal (ag) Mr. David McCarthy, wrote me a letter of appreciation a few weeks after I left the school as shown below:

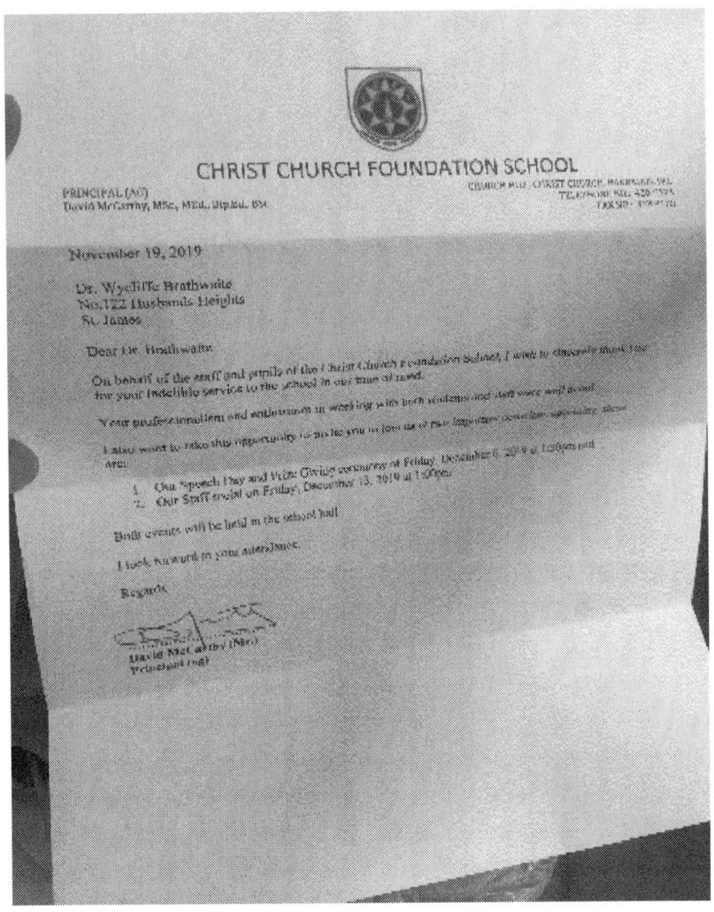

CHRIST CHURCH FOUNDATION SCHOOL

PRINCIPAL (AG)
David McCarthy, MSc, MEd., Dip.Ed., BSc

November 19, 2019

Dr. Wycliffe Brathwaite
No.122 Husbands Heights
St. James

Dear Dr. Brathwaite

On behalf of the staff and pupils of the Christ Church Foundation School, I wish to sincerely thank you for your indelible service to the school in our time of need.

Your professionalism and enthusiasm in working with both students and staff were well noted.

I also want to take this opportunity to invite you to join us at [illegible]

1. Our Speech Day and Prize Giving ceremony on Friday, December 6, 2019 at 1:30pm [illegible]
2. Our Staff social on Friday, December 13, 2019 at 1:30pm

Both events will be held in the school hall.

I look forward to your attendance.

Regards

David McCarthy (Mr.)
Principal (ag)

## Covid-19

March of 2020 epitomized the title of this book: "***Blowing Through the Thick Black Smoke***".

I was engaged in the teaching of a few courses at Barbados Community College: Music History 2. Improvisation, Jazz Ensemble along with tutoring three trumpet players. As I was in the process of administering exams for my students, everything changed with the advent of a viral disease that caught the entire world by surprise called, the Corona virus or Covid-19. I was also in collaboration with a British agent who was interested in organizing a few performing tours on my behalf. This was all put on the back burner. Teaching most courses from home via online became the new normal. My ensemble was one of the courses that suffered as a result. Teaching these courses online presented a completely new set of unforeseen challenges. Some students had connectivity issues. Everybody was forced to work from home, while other issues concerning family members surfaced. Managing all of these issues and students who once used studying as a getaway from home struggles became prevalent. Tutoring became a counseling chore. This was in tandem with managing my own resources at home, where two laptops had to be shared between my daughter, son and myself.

These issues were further compounded by a new protocol system of how the populace was to travel around during a daily curfew, which was mandated by government between 6 a.m. and 5 p.m. Not to mention that my son and daughter, both students, also had a fair share of daily online commitments as well. Hotels were shutdown, along with all other places of entertainment. This put a tremendous strain on the entire entertainment fraternity, worldwide. This strain was on not only entertainers and sports persons, who were losing their jobs at an alarming rate, but for live performing musicians and entertainers.

The Barbados annual music festival – 'Crop Over' - on which most musicians, music producers, arrangers, recording studios, costume designers, depended on for survival, was cancelled to mitigate the spread of the virus. This was probably the blackest smoke experienced during that period in my life as a musician, producer, educator, husband and father.

This experience was not unique to me. Musician friends in Germany and the USA, whom I had not heard from in years, were frequently contacting me either via social media or by telephone. A few of them actually sounded suicidal. Even though I may have developed some form of mental illness myself, I had to be strong for them. Suffice it to say, that once curfews were lifted and the world managed to resume some level of normalcy, I have not heard from those 'friends' since.

Despite all of the odds, I would not trade any of the individual aspects of my life as a professional trumpet player, arranger, producer, teacher, tutor, lecturer, composer, songwriter, entertainment manager, doctor, dad and husband, for the world!

God has been good and continues to be…

# Chapter 18

## Justice of The Peace [J.P.]

[State House: Nov. 21, 2024]

While completing the contents of this book, which, initially was supposed to be seventeen chapters, I thought it necessary to add a short eighteenth chapter to this memoir. Why? I got an unexpected call from the office of the Barbados Cabinet stating that I was recommended for the role of Justice of The Peace. It was stated that the recommendation had come from Government Minister, the Honorable, Sandra Husbands. It was a pleasant surprise.

I do not take this achievement lightly, because I was told by the Cabinet Secretary that this was a warrant issued by the President of Barbados on the recommendation of the Prime Minister to persons of unquestionable integrity. This is why it is so significant to me, because this is how I have always tried to live my life, despite pushback from several fronts in my quest to always hold myself to the highest possible standards.

I was sworn in and installed at State House by Her Excellency, Dame Sandra Mason, President of Barbados, on November 21, 2024 as a new JP.

There is no greater way to complete 18 chapters of a mere glimpse of my professional career thus far. I want to thank everyone who buys this book or took the time to read it.

THANK YOU!

## Edited Discography

List of Popular Songs Arranged/Produced

- *Gabby's Controversy - Grynner ( 1984 )*
- *Stinging Bees - Grynner ( 1984 )*
- *Sousie - Director ( 1985 )*
- *They Want To Know - Bumba ( 1987 )*
- *Wind Force - Gabby (1998)*
- *Bow Wow Wow - Carew ( 1988 )*
- *Faces - Lord Radio ( 1988 )*
- *Where The Good Men Gone - Marcie ( 1989 )*
- *Through It All - Joseph Niles ( 1989 )*
- *Fire - Kim Dereck ( 1989 )*
- *Ship Ahoy - Joseph Niles ( 1989 )*
- *Damage - Observer ( 1992 )*
- *Fantasy - David Hunte ( 1992 )*
- *Shuffle - Observer ( 1994 )*
- *Esterlyn – Centipede (1999)*
- *Cat-Astrophe – Smokey Burke (2007)*
- *Vote For DLP – Lil' Rick (2008)*
- *Inclusion In Reverse -- Collin Spencer (2009)*
- *Obama Kill Osama – Mighty Gabby (2011)*
- *Gone To Paris – Classic (2012)*
- *Sweetness -- Ian Webster (2012)*

- *Wait – Smokey Burke (2012)*
- *Pan Tuk – Chrystal Cummins-Beckles (2014)*
- *One People, One Nation – Aziza (2016)*
- *One Last Vote – Colin Spencer (2017)*
- *Shirley – Colin Sencer  (2015)*
- *A Poor Trait -- Smokey Burke (2017)*
- *We Still Standing Talk – Aziza (2017)*
- *PJ – Douchey (2018)*

## **Edited List of Caribbean Artists Recorded With** [Barbados]

- *Mighty Gabby*
- *Mighty Grynner*
- *Invader #3*
- *Classic*
- *Aziza*
- *Colin Spencer*
- *Brian "Bumba" Payne*
- *Smokey Burke*
- *Director - Sousie*
- *Mac Fingall*
- *Serenader*
- *Black Pawn*
- *IWeb  - Diabetes*
- *Observer - Damage*

## [Trinidad & Tobago]

- *Super Blue*
- *Mighty Sparrow*
- *Charlie's Roots: De Hammer (David Rudder)*
- *Charlie's Roots: Bahaia Girl (David Rudder)*
- *Denese Pumber*
- *Barron*
- *Roots Man*
- *Crazy*
- *Boogsey Sharp*
- *Mighty Trini*
- *Chalk Dust*

## [St. Vincent]

- *Beckette*
- *Soca Pat*
- *D'Rebel Band*
- *Touch*

## [St. Lucia]

- Lucian Parrot
- David "Chain" Aban

[Grenada]

- Ajamu

[Guyana]

- *Eddy Grant*

[Monserrat]

- Arrow -

[Martinique]

- Malavoi Orchestra
- West Indian Jazz Band

ORIGINAL COMPOSITIONS RECORDED & PRODUCED

- *Xmas Time (Vocal) 1983*
- *Hopping Mad (Vocal) 1990*
- *Where Are Your Roots (Vocal) 1990*
- *Soca Cha Cha (Vocal) 1990*
- *Play Mass (Vocal) 1991*
- *Supa Saf CD (solo Tpt album) 1998*
- *Sunflower CD (solo Tpt album) 2006*
- *City Life CD (solo Tpt album) 2012*
- *Music Video – 'Round Bridgetown 2014*
- *Single – "Love" (Vocal) 2018*

## Arrangements of Winning Calypso Monarchs

Brian “Bumba” Payne: (1997)

- “They want To Know”
- “Love Your Own”

Aziza: (2016)

- “One People, One Nation”
- “Bring Back Respect”

William “Classic” Waithe: (2019)

- “One Song”

Below are just a few snap shots of various News Paper articles capturing my musical journey over the years -- the last one being the most recent (July, 2024).

The writing of this memoir has brought tremendous pleasure in revisiting my musical journey from the tender age of 15, as a member of the Barbados Police Force Band, to the present – 2024.

I hope you have enjoyed reading it as much as I have enjoyed writing and presenting it to you. Unfortunately, I could only provide a few of the many News Paper clips secured over several decades -- many undergone the natural process of deterioration.

Ricky B awarded scholarship

Gabby, Squa[r]... caught in Cro...

Ricky's talent trumpets forth

WEEKEND MAGAZINE

FREE PULL-OUT

RICKY BRATHWAITE: All-round musician

Together

PARTY SCENE

Hot cup

10

# Ricky blowing a different tune

TOP trumpeter Ricky Brathwaite has hit a high note.

Two weeks ago, the Berklee-trained musician took up the post of production director at Rainbow/WIRL.

"We were thinking about this for a long time and had a need for someone with this kind of [illegible]. He is outstanding in his field, so the [illegible]" said Rainbow/WIRL general manager [illegible] yesterday.

"The company has [illegible] staff. He comes [illegible] bring [illegible]" [illegible] added.

TOP TRUMPETER Ricky Brathwaite recently [illegible] new post at Rainbow/WIRL.

FRIDAY, AUGUST 25, 1995

SHOWTIME • SHOWTIME • SHOWTIME

olut-ly

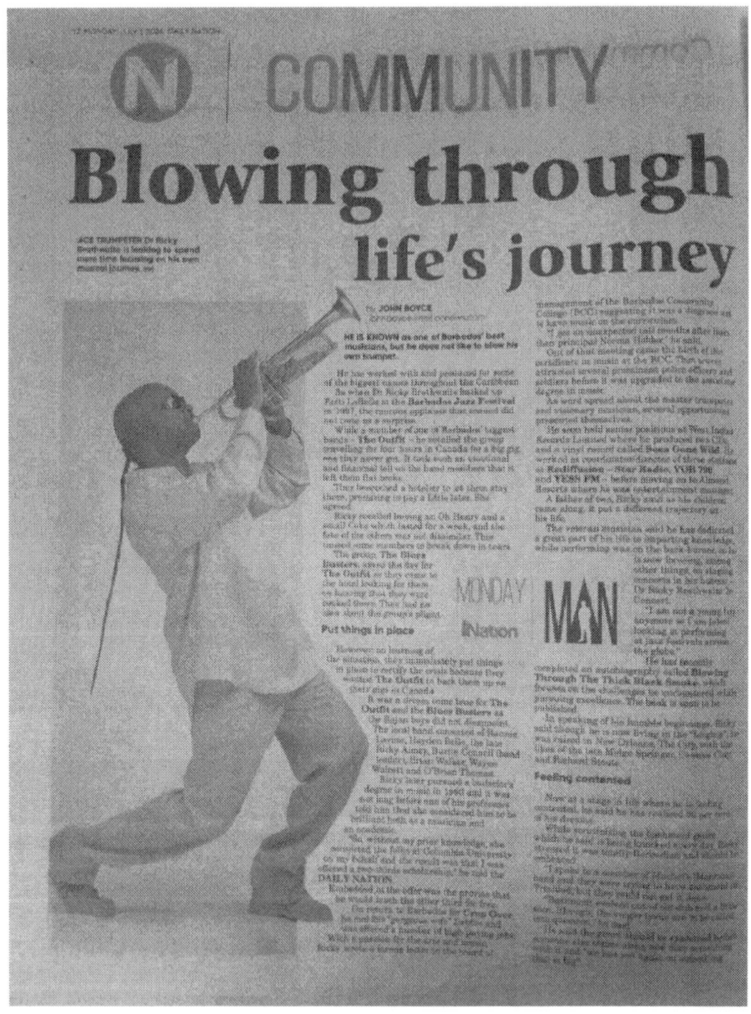

COMMUNITY

# Blowing through life's journey

by JOHN BOYCE

HE IS KNOWN as one of Barbados' best musicians, but he does not like to blow his own trumpet.

MONDAY MAN

Nation

Put things in place

Feeling contented

Made in the USA
Middletown, DE
25 February 2025

71789125R00122